THE GOLDEN CENTURY
England Under the Tudors

From 1485 to 1603, England was ruled by the Tudors—a bizarre assortment of three kings and three queens. Henry VII, the first Tudor monarch, united his kingdom and restored its prosperity after the divisive Wars of the Roses. He was followed by the ruthless Henry VIII, whose unchecked appetites led to the Reformation; young Edward VI, pawn of wicked nobles; pathetic Lady Jane Grey; and the infamous "bloody" Mary I. This vital century, which ended in a burst of glory under Queen Elizabeth I, marked the end of the feudal era and the beginning of the modern age.

Books by
CLIFFORD LINDSEY ALDERMAN

The
Golden Century

England Under the Tudors

CLIFFORD LINDSEY ALDERMAN

photographs

Julian
Messner

New York

Published by Julian Messner
a division of Simon & Schuster, Inc.
1 West 39th Street, New York, N.Y. 10018
All Rights Reserved

Printed in the United States of America

ISBN 0-671-32514-0 Cloth Trade
0-671-32515-9 MCE

Library of Congress Catalog Card No. 74-182946

11-5-'73

CONTENTS

58093

1

How the Tudors Changed England

FOR MORE THAN A CENTURY, from 1485 to 1603, England was ruled by the Tudors—first by three kings, then by three queens. Their influence on England was immense. Their coming marked the end of thirty years of civil war in England; the end of the Tudor period saw the country advanced to new greatness and such prosperity as it had never known before.

The Tudor rulers were as different as six members of the same royal lineage could be. Of the three kings, the first one alone, Henry VII, can truly be called great, even though he is not the best known of them. Save for a few quickly suppressed rebellions and attempted foreign invasions of England, inspired by English rebels, Henry VII kept England at peace, made the kingdom financially sound, started it on the road to prosperity and gave the common man a real chance to improve himself.

Though Henry VII's son and successor, Henry VIII, is probably the most famous of English kings, he cannot be called good or great. He squandered the wealth his father had accumulated. He flew into terrible rages, punished his enemies without mercy, ruled as a dictator, married six wives and beheaded two of them. He got England into wasteful foreign wars. Most important of all, he threw the country into turmoil by a quarrel with the Pope that changed England from a Roman Catholic nation to one whose religion was controlled by himself alone, thereby causing untold trouble in the future and altering the course of English history.

The third Tudor monarch, poor Edward VI, came to the throne at nine and died at fifteen. During his short reign, England was ruled first by a Protector, overambitious for power, then by one of the wickedest men who ever lived in England. Edward VI had almost no chance to do what he wanted most—to improve the life of the wretched poor and to become the good king he could have been.

Then came the first queen. Lady Jane Grey is to be pitied too. She was thrust upon a throne she did not want by her vicious parents and the evil nobleman who had dominated Edward VI's last days. She was never crowned, reigned only nine days and had no influence on English history.

Queen Mary I, her successor, wanted and tried to be a good queen, but instead she became infamous for her fanatical devotion to her Catholic religion. During her reign the block on the green of the Tower of London and the scaffold on Tower Hill were soaked with blood that flowed under the headsman's ax, not to mention the hundreds burned at the stake for refusing to give up their Protestant faith.

The next and last of the Tudors was Elizabeth I, generally considered to be the greatest queen England ever had. She ended the mischief Mary I had caused, and proved herself a true granddaughter of Henry VII by saving the kingdom money and bringing it greater prosperity. She kept England almost completely out of foreign wars and was a genius at politics and foreign policy. She ruled strictly, sometimes harshly, but was loved by the people as no other ruler before her had been. Here, indeed, was a mighty queen.

Thus the era of the Tudors was notable. True, there were wars, and only one resulted in good for England—the disastrous defeat of the Spanish Armada in 1588 during Elizabeth's reign, ending a serious threat by Spain to invade and conquer England. One other war, under Mary I, was a disaster for England. It resulted in the loss of Calais, her last foothold in a France that had once been largely under English control, only to be lost, little by little, over the centuries. And there were conspiracies and rebellions; a few were serious, although all were crushed, most of them quickly.

But such lamentable events were overbalanced, during the 118-year rule of the Tudors, by changes for good. The greatest gain was that England, being at peace during most of the period, became prosperous, and for the first time many of the common people were able to improve their way of life, have a real voice in the government and often become wealthy and even titled. A look at England in the time of the Tudors, and a few stories of humble men who achieved prosperity, wealth and high rank will illustrate what happened.

Peter Blundell was born in the town of Tiverton, in the southwest of England, in Devonshire, in 1520. Since 1509 Henry VIII had been on the throne, but Henry VII's great changes for the better had already been taking place in England.

Unfortunately, these changes did not improve the fortunes of everyone, including Peter Blundell's parents. Although little is

9

known of them, they were poor. True, the old villeinage, or serfdom—the system under which peasants were enslaved by the landlords for whom they worked in order to be allowed to support themselves by farming a strip of the lord's land—was practically gone. Peter Blundell's parents doubtless paid rent to the lord of a manor for the land they farmed.

But the wool and cloth trade was now the most profitable one in England. An enormous amount of land had been enclosed by hedges; where crops had once grown, vast herds of sheep now grazed. However, Peter Blundell's parents were either too poor to buy sheep and raise wool or perhaps too old-fashioned to change their way of life.

Fine, large new houses of heavy timber and stone were being built all over England by those who were making large profits from the country's new prosperity. But Peter Blundell's house was probably the old "wattle-and-daub," built of wooden posts holding walls of interwoven twigs filled with mud or clay and having a thatched roof.

Such houses usually had only one room, a floor of hard-packed earth, windows without glass and a hole in the roof that let out at least some of the smoke from the fireplace. The furniture was crude—a table of boards that could be placed on a trestle support, stools to sit on, straw or rushes for beds, a few metal or clay pots and other utensils for cooking, wooden trenchers for plates and wooden noggins for cups.

The food was simple but good, and there was usually plenty of it. Beef was cheap and the bread, made from rye or barley, nourishing, though not like the wheat bread baked in small loaves called manchets and eaten by the rich. And there was plenty of home-brewed beer.

But as a boy, Peter might have remembered bad seasons when poor people made their bread from horse corn, peas, beans, oats, the tares or vetches ordinarily used to feed livestock, lentils and even, in especially hard times, from acorns.

Although there is no record that Peter ever had any education, he was smart. He became aware of the changes that were taking place. Although Tiverton was thriving because of the wool and cloth trade, many villages were losing population as people moved to towns and cities where new industries were being established and good jobs were plentiful. Felt, thread, lace, parchment, needles and glass were being made, and of course there was England's best trade, the cloth industry.

Peter understood that now a poor, uneducated peasant boy could make something of himself if he could obtain enough money to start his own business. So young Peter began to run errands for people in Tiverton. It didn't pay much, but he saved every penny he could of what he earned.

One day someone said to him, "You're an ambitious boy, Peter. I hear they need an hostler at the inn. Why don't you have a try at it? 'Twill pay better than running errands."

Peter went there immediately and convinced the innkeeper he could care for horses properly. He was put to work tending, feeding, watering and currying the mounts of guests who stopped overnight at the inn. He worked hard and diligently, using his currycomb on the animals' coats until they shone. Now that he was earning regular wages, he could save more.

Peter began to think of what business he should go into. The most profitable one in Tiverton was in kerseys. Kersey was a light-weight woolen cloth, woven and finished with such skill that it had a smooth surface and was soft to the touch. Kerseys were

11

made in Devonshire, but to sell them one had to get them to London, where the market was so good that profits of 100 per cent were often made.

Peter now had enough money to buy some kerseys, but the problem was to get them to London. Dealers sent kerseys there by carriers, who usually joined a pack train of horses for greater safety against robbers on the roads. From Tiverton a carrier would go a few miles south to Exeter over one of the deeply rutted tracks that were little more than trails. Through Exeter ran one of the main roads to London, somewhat better going, although even such highways in England at that time were unpaved, full of holes and dusty in dry weather and boggy in wet.

To carry his kerseys to London would require a horse, and Peter owned none and could not afford to hire one. But he had become friendly with one of the kersey carriers who was often at the inn. "If I bought some kerseys, would you take them to London for me and sell them?" he asked the man.

"Aye," said the carrier, "I'll bear 'em there for you and sell 'em."

"How much will you charge me?"

"Why," said the carrier, "you're a good lad, Peter, and you take good care of my horses. It'll cost you naught."

The carrier, an honest man, was as good as his word. He took the kerseys Peter bought with his little store of savings, sold them in London and turned all the profits over to the young man.

After that, as he kept shipping kerseys to London, Peter was able to pay the carrier. Finally he had the money to buy a full load of kerseys and a pack horse. He had decided to take the cloth to London himself.

The journey of close to two hundred miles must have been

one of the great experiences of Peter Blundell's young life. He saw new country, towns and cities and learned much he had not known of life and trade in other parts of England. Bad as the road was, there were plenty of good inns where he could enjoy a comfortable bed and excellent food at a low price. Prosperous people he met and talked with gave Peter new inspiration to succeed.

Of course, the journey was dangerous. The vast, rolling moorlands of Salisbury Plain teemed with lurking highwaymen, but Peter came through safely. The countryside was fascinating; walking beside his full-laden pack horse, he may have gazed in awe at the mysterious stone structures of Stonehenge on the plain, and also, when he reached the valley of the Thames River, at Windsor Castle, for two hundred years one of the residences of English kings and queens.

Then—London. Peter must have been astonished at the size and splendor of the mighty city. He entered through one of the gates in the walls the invading Romans had built in the second century, still standing but not kept repaired and beginning to crumble. The rattle and rumble of the traffic in the narrow streets and the great crush of people were frightening at first. Finally, walking along, he reached West Cheap, or Cheapside, where he had been told he could find dealers in kerseys. It was not only the broadest street in London, but the city's great market, lined on both sides with shops of all kinds.

Peter reached the section where merchant tailors had their establishments. He drove a shrewd bargain with one, and exchanged his kerseys for coins that clinked merrily in his pocket. Then he sought out an inn and put up for the night.

He spent a day or so exploring the city. Along the bank of the

13

Thames he gazed at the great town houses of the rich and wondered if a country boy like himself could ever own one. In the river so many ships rode at anchor that their bare masts looked like a fire-swept forest, and Peter realized that here lay the secret of London's prosperity—trade. And there was the marvel of London Bridge, one of the wonders of the world.

From Ludgate Hill, where stood the immense cathedral of St. Paul's, Peter could see the grim walls of the Tower of London, enclosing the White Tower and other buildings, and in the opposite direction, along the Thames and outside the city walls, Westminster, the heart of England's government, and Whitehall Palace.

Strolling into St. Paul's, Peter was shocked to find its vast nave filled with a rabble. There were "shopkeepers" who used tombs as counters to display their goods, scriveners who wrote letters for the uneducated, lounging, well-dressed merchants and nobles and groups of lawyers discussing their cases. Balladmongers added to the pandemonium by bawling their songs amid a horde of beggars, who claimed to be shipwrecked sailors, or lame, blind or homeless after their houses and belongings had been destroyed by fire. Even a countryman like Peter could see that most of them were frauds, and although he did not know it, the nave also teemed with slick-fingered pickpockets and other thieves.

Peter saw real want in some of the narrow streets, lined with ramshackle rookeries where the very poor lived, turning these lanes into pigsties with the rubbish and garbage they threw into them. In the gutters ran little rivers of sewage, and the nearest thing to garbage collectors were the kites and ravens, the city's scavengers.

Yet London was most attractive—a flourishing, busy place that offered all sorts of opportunities for an ambitious young fellow. Peter made a decision: he would remain there and find work in the kersey manufacturing trade. He was successful in obtaining employment with a merchant who dealt in kerseys. As he had done in Tiverton, Peter saved his money until he was able to establish his own business as a kersey manufacturer.

After some years, Peter was so well off that this son of poor parents could sign his name: "Peter Blundell, gent.," since he was now entitled to call himself a gentleman. And since he had plenty of money, he began to think of the joys of rural living amid green meadows, forests and sparkling streams. He decided to sell his business, return to Tiverton and live as a country gentleman.

He was glad to be home, but after the excitements of London he found life dull in a Devonshire town that would have been swallowed up if put down in the great city of London. He finally returned to the metropolis to spend the rest of his days.

Peter Blundell must have become an important and influential man in London, for when he died in 1601 he named his "right deare and honourable friende, Sir John Popham, Lord Chief Justice of England," to carry out the terms of his will. In it he did not forget Tiverton, for he left most of his money to found a free school there for 150 scholars, as well as a fund to maintain forever six students of divinity at either Oxford or Cambridge universities.

Other men rose from a lowly state to wealth and power. Little is known of the Bale family before it came to Carlton Curlieu in Leicestershire. Presumably the Bales' ancestors had been serfs. When John Bale came to Carlton Curlieu in the reign of Henry

VIII, he was a yeoman—a freeholder who owned land of his own.

Land was the best investment in England, since with sheep raising and woolen manufacturing increasing, grazing land's value also increased. In 1549 John Bale bought two farms in Carlton Curlieu from the Earl of Huntingdon. As the style of living in England under the Tudors became more luxurious, the great lords often found themselves in need of cash and were willing to sell part of their great estates, and thrifty yeomen like John Bale could buy the land.

Some years later, in 1558, John Bale bought four hundred more acres in nearby Burton Overy. He bought several hundred more in 1562 and 1563 in Carlton Curlieu and neighboring parishes. Then, in 1570, John Bale died, wealthy enough so that while he still described himself as a yeoman, he might, like Peter Blundell, have signed himself "gent.," as one of the gentry.

John Bale had no children, and he left his lands to his nephew, also named John Bale. The younger Bale, who did call himself "gent.," was as smart and shrewd as his uncle. In 1575 he bought the entire manor of Carlton Curlieu from its lord, as well as six hundred more acres of land. By 1590 he owned the whole parish of Carlton Curlieu.

The first of the Stuart kings was on the throne when the younger Bale died in 1622. He was then Sir John Bale, having been knighted by James I, and owned thousands of acres of land. Thus, during the Tudor period, another English family rose from humble beginnings to wealth and later to knighthood, something almost impossible in medieval times.

In the cities, too, poor boys could rise to wealth and titles. Edward Osburne, who had been an apprentice to a merchant,

Sir William Hewet, not only was rich and titled, but had served as Lord Mayor of London in 1559.

Sir William Hewet lived on London Bridge. It seems queer to think of living on a bridge, but many prosperous people did. It was crowded on both sides by a hodgepodge of houses and expensive shops. Their upper stories jutted out over the roadway in the center, making it almost like a tunnel. It was hardly recognizable as a bridge in the sixteenth century except that it spanned the Thames.

As was often the case with apprentices, Edward Osburne lived in his master's house on the bridge, though under the lowliest of conditions. The water below was tempestuous, since the twenty arches of the bridge narrowed the current. One day, a servant girl accidentally let Sir William's infant daughter fall into the churning maelstrom of black water below through an open window. Instantly, Edward Osburne dived in. He was a powerful swimmer, but he had a desperate struggle and was almost drowned before he brought the baby to safety.

From that day on, Edward Osburne was considered one of the Hewet family. Meanwhile, Sir William's little daughter grew into a lovely young girl. She had many titled suitors, but Sir William would have none of them.

"Osburne saved her!" he cried. "None but Osburne shall have her."

And so they were married, and her father gave her a rich dowry. Edward's apprenticeship ended, and he became a merchant in the cloth trade and a member of the Clothworkers' Company, one of the powerful guilds something like the unions of today. The Lord Mayor of London was always chosen from a guild, and Edward Osburne not only became Lord Mayor, but was knighted. Luck, as well as courage, played a part in his rise to prosperity and high standing, but before the Tudors it was most unlikely that it could have happened.

This was the greatest accomplishment of the Tudor era—the advancement of the common man. It had already begun when the first of the six Tudors, Henry VII, came to the throne, but he gave it a strong push ahead. Under his successors England's prosperity did not advance as quickly, but with the last and most glorious of all, Elizabeth I, it leaped ahead again.

The Tudor age was remarkable in other ways—some good, some bad. It was a time of prosperity for the most part, an age of great men in literature, trade, government, diplomacy and exploration and discovery. On the other hand, it was a time of war and the bloody violence of two rulers and, most important, of the Reformation—the bitter, shattering strife between the Church in England and the Church of Rome.

Three kings and three queens. Three—one king and two queens—are among the most famous of all English rulers for their deeds, good and evil. The first Tudor, Henry VII, is less famous, yet he set England on a course toward greatness that was to come to its height three centuries later in the powerful, world-wide British Empire.

2

The King Without a Face

HENRY VII OF ENGLAND WAS A GREAT KING, but little is known of the man himself—only his deeds. He has been called the king without a face. But the two or three portraits of him all have certain revealing features—the thin lips that can be a sign of meanness, and the hooded eyes, with a cunning, penetrating and distrustful look.

He had no real friends except perhaps his uncle, Jasper Tudor, without whose staunch support Henry would probably never have been King. And Henry's subjects did not love him, even though the King used pawns to carry out some of his unpopular measures, especially the collection of heavy taxes. The English people loved his Queen, Elizabeth of York, and his little son, Arthur. But Henry VII's public appearances brought few cheers or other expressions of affection.

Yet despite his unpopularity and his meanness in some ways, he was a very great ruler. He took his kingdom out of the slough of medieval tyranny, taking away much of the power of the great, landowning lords and giving it to the common people.

When Henry VII assumed the crown, England was torn and gasping for life after the off-and-on, thirty-year struggle for control of the country known as the Wars of the Roses. He put the nation back on its feet, filled its almost empty treasury, restored a system of justice to a realm that had almost forgotten what law and order were like, brought back thriving trade, erected many imposing buildings, established schools and colleges and did many other things to revive England and put it on a course toward future greatness.

A noted historian believes that Henry VII has a claim as the greatest of all the Tudors, even though that honor is generally given to Elizabeth I.

Henry VII had little or no preparation that enabled him to take over a strife-torn, poverty-stricken nation and restore it to peace and prosperity. He did have royal blood—English from his mother, who had been Margaret Beaufort, a great-granddaughter of King Edward III; French from his father, Edmund Tudor, whose mother was Catherine of Valois, daughter of a French king.

Just before Henry's birth, his father, the Earl of Richmond, had died in prison, a victim of the Wars of the Roses, and his mother had fled to refuge in Wales. There Henry was born on January 28, 1457. By inheritance, Henry was Earl of Richmond.

He might just as well have been an orphan, for before he was four years old his mother married again and went blithely off to live with her new husband, leaving Henry in the care of his uncle, Jasper Tudor, the Earl of Pembroke. So he seems to have had little of the motherly love most children enjoy.

Soon after Henry's mother left him he was separated from his uncle too. The Wars of the Roses were still raging. For the time being, the Yorkist side was triumphant and the Yorkist King Edward IV had come to the throne. Since Jasper Tudor was on the Lancastrian side, the Yorkists captured his castle of Pembroke. Jasper managed to escape and flee to Scotland, but young Henry was captured.

Jasper's title of Earl of Pembroke was taken from him and given to Lord William Herbert, who was appointed young Henry's guardian. What the little boy's life was like as a prisoner of the new earl is not known, but it must have been most unhappy, for he spoke bitterly of it in later years.

Since Jasper Tudor was an exile from England, sure to be beheaded if he came back and was captured, he wandered about Scotland for a time and then, for greater safety, went to France. All the while he was watching for a chance to rescue his nephew, young Henry. In 1469, when the boy was twelve, Edward's army was routed by the Lancastrians near Banbury and the King was captured.

The Lancastrian King Henry VI, ousted from the throne by Edward IV, was restored. Jasper Tudor promptly returned to Wales and took Henry from Lady Herbert, who was in charge of him then, since her husband had been captured at Banbury and beheaded. Jasper then took Henry to London and presented him to the restored King.

Henry VI, a good and pious but weak man, did have keen foresight when he said, after he had received Henry Tudor: "This truly, this is he unto whom both we and our adversaries must yield and give over to domination." The prophecy would come true.

First, however, more trouble lay ahead for Jasper and Henry Tudor. In 1471 a Lancastrian army led by Henry VI's warlike and dauntless wife, Margaret of Anjou, was cut to pieces at the battle of Tewkesbury. Edward IV regained the throne, and poor Henry VI went to the Tower of London, where he was to die a prisoner. Jasper Tudor and his nephew barely escaped capture by the victorious Yorkists. They managed to flee to the duchy of Brittany, on the west coast of what is now France.

Duke Francis II of Brittany received them hospitably, but he knew that in young Henry Tudor he had a very valuable prize. Edward IV, aware that Henry had a claim to the throne, was itching to get his hands on the boy. He began to negotiate with Francis II to surrender Henry to him. He promised to marry Henry to his daughter Elizabeth; in that way, Lancaster and York would be united and the Wars of the Roses might end.

During Henry Tudor's years of exile in Brittany, he and his uncle seem to have lived comfortably, though always fearful of what might become of them if Duke Francis yielded to Edward IV's persuasions. And Henry did have tutors, thus at least getting an education in preparation for the future.

Then came some terrifying days for Henry Tudor. Duke Francis decided to give him up to Edward IV. He handed the young man over to Edward's emissaries, and they set off for Saint Malo. But when they reached this seaport and were about to embark for England, a troop of Breton soldiers charged in, headed by the duke's treasurer, Pierre Landois. Duke Francis had changed his mind. There was nothing the English envoys could do but accept Landois's promise that the duke would make sure Henry did not escape from Brittany.

Now Henry was a prisoner. But in 1483 Edward IV died, and after that Henry's confinement was relaxed. However, the new King of England, Richard III, who had seized the crown illegally, knew full well that Henry Tudor was the most serious menace to his unsteady throne.

The Duke of Buckingham, a close but treacherous friend of Richard III, also knew this. He plotted a revolt to put Henry

Tudor on the throne. Henry was willing, and sailed with a force to invade England and join Buckingham. Fortunately, a storm drove his ships back to Brittany, for Buckingham's revolt failed and he was captured and beheaded.

Richard III was rid of his false friend, but now he bent all his efforts toward getting hold of Henry Tudor. He tried in vain to bribe Duke Francis into handing Henry over to him, but then the duke suddenly became insane. Pierre Landois, an unscrupulous man, saw in Francis' mental illness a chance to make a great deal of money for himself. He accepted Richard's offer in the name of the duke.

However, one of the conspirators in Buckingham's plot had escaped to Flanders. He learned of what Landois intended to do and sent a warning to Henry Tudor. Henry then obtained permission from King Charles VIII of France to take refuge there.

Henry and his faithful uncle laid careful plans to escape without attracting Landois's attention. Jasper announced that he was going to pay a visit to the ailing Duke Francis, who was at Vannes, in the direction of the French border. To lull Landois's suspicions, Jasper took most of the two Tudors' followers with him, but left Henry behind. Two days later, Henry made a dash for freedom, accompanied by five servants. In a wood a short distance away, he changed clothes with one of the servants. Then, taking a zigzag route to throw pursuers off the trail, he began a reckless gallop for the French frontier.

Landois quickly discovered that the bird had flown. A troop of his horsemen were close on Henry's heels when he reached the border and crossed to safety in France, where his uncle awaited him.

Now Henry Tudor was ready for the greatest adventure of his life. Many gentry of the west country who wanted the usurper

Richard III ousted from the throne had crossed to Brittany to join Henry. He managed to borrow some money and obtain some ships, and on August 1, 1485, he sailed from Harfleur with about two thousand men.

He landed in Wales, catching Richard by surprise. By the time the King heard of it, Henry and his uncle were marching eastward across England, reinforced by many loyal Welshmen and picking up English supporters on the way.

Richard hastily assembled an army and set out to intercept the invaders. They met at Bosworth Field in the Midlands of England. In this desperate, greatest and last battle of the Wars of the Roses, Richard III was slain and his army put to flight. The golden crown he had worn into battle toppled off his head as he fought single-handedly against the enemies who had closed in around him. Battered and mud-stained, it was recovered and, just outside the battlefield, placed on the head of Henry Tudor, who was hailed as King Henry VII of England.

Henry VII was officially crowned with the usual great pomp and ceremony in Westminster Abbey on October 30, 1485. His first and most important objective was to heal the wounds of the Wars of the Roses by uniting the two enemy houses of Lancaster and York. Then he could start to improve a nation that was torn from north to south and east to west, poverty-stricken and lawless.

Henry called a Parliament to meet a week later. Meanwhile, he appointed both Lancastrians and Yorkists to high government posts. His first Chancellor, the highest-ranking government official, had been one of the Yorkist King Edward IV's chancellors. Another high official, the Lord Privy Seal, had once been Edward IV's secretary. And other Yorkists were named to responsible positions.

Not forgetting the Lancastrians who had put him on the throne, Henry appointed his faithful uncle, Jasper Tudor, as Duke of Bedford. Lord Thomas Stanley and his brother Sir William, who had turned the tide in Henry Tudor's favor by coming to his aid at Bosworth Field, were also remembered. Sir William became Earl of Derby, and Lord Thomas was appointed Lord Chamberlain, in charge of the royal household.

Henry VII restored the lands and estates of many rich Lancastrians that had been seized by the Yorkists. However, some of the great landowners had been killed in the wars or had died leaving no heirs. Henry VII's first Parliament granted him these properties, something he needed badly for their revenues, since his own privy purse, like the country's treasury, was nearly empty.

Henry's next move was to bring peace and unity between the two great houses by fulfilling his promise to marry Edward IV's daughter, Elizabeth of York. This he did on January 18, 1486.

Next the King set out on a progress to the north, for that wild and often lawless part of England had been a Yorkist stronghold during the Wars of the Roses. A progress, used to advantage by many English rulers, was simply a leisurely journey through some part of the kingdom so that the people could see their kings and queens in all their royal magnificence. If the sovereigns also showed themselves as kindly people who had come to see their subjects because they were really interested in their welfare, they might expect love and loyalty in return. At the same time, the rulers could take along a powerful, fully armed escort to put fear into the hearts of rebellious men who might be plotting an uprising.

Henry VII's first progress was a success. A young man of twenty-nine, he was tall and slender, well built and strong, with golden hair. And while he did not have the magnetism that immediately attracted people and gained their instant loyalty and devotion, for the most part great crowds received him cordially with expressions of goodwill all along his route, even in the city of York, long a center of loyalty to the Yorkists.

Nevertheless, in the early years of his reign, Henry had to put down several revolts before he could be sure that he was practically in control of his entire kingdom. One of these uprisings came during Henry's first progress. When he reached Lincoln, in mideastern England, he was informed that a band of Richard III's most loyal followers was lurking on the road ahead, waiting to spring from hiding and kill him.

The smart young King wanted no bloodshed to mar the beginning of his reign and perhaps turn others against him. He summoned the leader of a force of his horsemen.

"Ride ahead, surprise the rebels and rout them out of their ambush," he commanded. "Offer them my full pardon if they will disperse peaceably. "

The cavalry rode off, took the concealed rebels by surprise and did as the King had ordered. Except for their leader, who escaped, the men, impressed by this show of strength, accepted the royal forgiveness and went home.

The next trouble of this sort might have been much more serious, but the ending turned out to be comical. When Edward IV died, he left two young sons. The elder boy became King Edward V, though he was never crowned. Instead, Edward's brother Richard, Duke of Gloucester, seized the throne as Richard III. Both the boy King and his younger brother, Prince Richard, next in line for the crown, were threats to Richard III. He managed to seize both boys and put them in the Tower of London. They were never seen outside it again.

Their fate is one of the great mysteries of English history. For years it was believed that Richard III had murdered them, or at least ordered them killed. But today historians are not so sure that Richard was responsible. There were others anxious to depose him and take the throne. These men might have arranged for the deaths of the little princes, as they are usually called.

But since in 1486 no one knew what the two boys' fate had been, a priest in Oxford, Richard Simonds, discovered a fine chance to improve his own fortunes by producing an impostor supposed to be the missing boy King, Edward V. A tradesman in Oxford had sent his son, Lambert Simnel, to the priest to be educated.

As he looked at the boy, it suddenly struck Simonds that Lambert resembled the missing sons of Edward IV. Why not train him in kingly ways and claim he was King Edward V? The priest could be sure of help from Henry VII's enemies, for in spite of all his efforts he still had them, both in England and abroad.

Simonds took Lambert Simnel to Ireland. The Irish, who bitterly hated England, were told that the Emerald Isle would regain its freedom if the impostor could sit on the English throne. Since 1171, when King Henry II of England had invaded Ireland, the people there had been cruelly oppressed by their English masters. They did not care whether Lambert Simnel was an impostor or not; this race of hard-fighting, brave, freedom-loving people would do anything to end the tyranny of England.

Over on the continent of Europe, Simnel had a powerful friend too. Dowager Duchess Margaret of Burgundy, a sister of Edward IV, hated Henry VII. She accepted Lambert Simnel as the missing young King and raised an army of two thousand German soldiers to invade England.

In England itself, in unruly Devonshire and Cornwall in the southwest, a group of rebellious nobles and gentry joined the plot. In Ireland the Earl of Lincoln, a nephew of Richard III, commanded the Irish army, which was also preparing to invade.

As reports from his spies reached him, Henry VII was greatly alarmed. Two invasions, one from the east and one from the west, threatened him. Expecting the landing of Margaret of Burgundy's troops first, Henry assembled an army and marched into East Anglia along the east coast. But the Earl of Lincoln landed his Irishmen first, marching eastward across the north of England into Yorkshire and then south towards London.

Lincoln's and Henry's armies met at Loughborough in Leicestershire. In a fierce three-hour battle in which four thousand men perished, most of them invaders, King Henry's men smashed the rebels. The Earl of Lincoln was killed, and young Lambert Simnel was captured.

Ordinarily, the impostor would have instantly been beheaded. But as has been said, Henry was a very smart ruler. Also, what he did gives another small glimpse into the character behind this faceless king—he could be humane. He gave Lambert Simnel a job as a turnspit in his kitchen. It was the lowliest of occupations—turning spits before the fires that roasted beef, mutton, venison and other meat. In fact, dogs were sometimes harnessed to turnstiles, walking around and around to turn the spits. England, from the wild moors of Yorkshire and Northumberland to the rolling downs of Kent, from the lonely marshlands of East Anglia to the rugged mountains of the west country, must have rocked with laughter when the people heard of it.

Nevertheless, Henry VII was still shaken over what might have been his downfall. He quickly made another gesture for Yorkist friendship. He had married Elizabeth of York as he had promised, but she had not been crowned. Now her coronation took place in spectacular fashion at Westminster Abbey.

For a time England was calm again, but in 1491 more serious trouble flared up. One would have thought anyone would have known better than to try the "impostor" game again, but another young man appeared, claiming he was Duke Richard, the younger of Edward IV's sons, the missing "little princes." It was really a fantastic business. The impostor this time was not even an Englishman, but from Brittany. His name was Perkin Warbeck (in Brittany it was spelled Warbecque).

Perkin Warbeck was a sailor aboard a Breton ship that sailed into Cork, Ireland. Unlike most horny-handed Breton seadogs, Perkin Warbeck was handsome, and had a regal appearance and charming manners. Some of the Irish leaders saw him and decided he was the very one to impersonate the missing Prince Richard. What matter that he did not speak English? He could be taught, and he was.

Perkin Warbeck then went to Burgundy to present himself to the Duchess Margaret as her nephew, Prince Richard. Whether Margaret believed him or not, she acknowledged him as the heir to the throne—since Richard's older brother, Edward V, appeared to be dead—and set about to help Perkin raise an army.

Henry VII got wind of the plan. Although he spoke scornfully of Perkin Warbeck, he was alarmed. There were English noblemen among Henry's enemies who were in the plot, and the King's spies dug up their names. One must have been a staggering blow to him. It was that of his own Lord Chamberlain, Sir William Stanley, who with his brother Lord Thomas, now Earl of Derby, had swung the victory to the Lancastrians at Bosworth Field and won Henry's crown for him.

Henry's rage must have been terrible indeed, for there was no actual proof that Sir William planned to revolt against the King. But this time Henry showed no mercy. Sir William and a number of others were arrested, condemned and executed.

In spite of this setback to his plans, Perkin Warbeck raised an army of between two and three thousand men and landed near the mouth of the Thames in 1495. Henry VII was waiting for him with a powerful force. All but about eighty in Perkin's army were killed, and the survivors captured and hanged.

But Perkin Warbeck himself escaped to Scotland, where King James IV accepted him as the missing prince. The Scottish King, no friend of England, then invaded England himself from the north, while Perkin Warbeck sailed around to Cornwall, farther from the Scottish border than any other part of England. Thus Henry VII would be beset from the far north and the far southwest at the same time.

Henry took care of James IV first and drove him back to Scotland. Then he and his army marched the length of England, close to three hundred miles, routed Warbeck's invaders and later captured the pretender. Again the King was humane enough to imprison him, but when Perkin escaped and was recaptured, he was promptly hanged. Henry VII had had enough of impostors, and decided to make an example of Warbeck to discourage others.

Never again during his reign did Henry have to put down a serious revolt or repel invaders. He made a move to insure peace with England's ancient enemy, Scotland, by marrying his daughter Margaret to the Scottish King. Even then it was an uneasy peace, but there was no real war. So now Henry VII could give his full attention to matters of state and steering England on a steady course towards well-being.

3

How Henry VII
Restored England

WHEN HENRY VII CAME TO THE THRONE, England badly needed three things: unity, money and a proper system of justice. He had accomplished the first, as nearly as unity could be achieved, though for many years after Henry's reign there would still be unruly parts of the kingdom in the wild country of the far north and west.

Meanwhile, Henry had begun his efforts to bring about the other two desirable objectives. The English treasury, all but empty, needed large sums of money to carry on the government. Also, the King's privy purse was in want of filling. It was his source of income to maintain his household and his palaces and to pay for his own style of living and enjoyment, his progresses and various other expenses.

With the Wars of the Roses over, the tremendous cost of fighting them was ended and the regular sources of government income could be used for other purposes. But this was not enough for Henry VII.

Early historians pictured Henry as greedy and claimed that

when he died he left £1,800,000, a fabulous fortune in those times. Modern historians dispute this and say that when he died his personal fortune was only enough to pay his funeral expenses. This did not include the jewels, gold and silver plate and other objects of value he owned, but such records as there are account for only about £140,000 spent for such things during his reign.

Henry did bring a great deal of money into the treasury and the privy purse. He spent his own lavishly and cleverly managed to divert much money directly into the privy purse that would otherwise have gone first into the public treasury, or Exchequer.

For a close-mouthed, reserved "king without a face," Henry lived in astonishing magnificence. He wore the richest clothes and saw to it that the nobles of his Court had the finest of silks, satins and velvets. He provided the best of food in great abundance, and spared no expense in building his new and favorite palace of Richmond and adding new, handsomely furnished buildings at other palaces where he spent much of his time. He loved hunting and hawking, which meant keeping stables of horses, many hunting dogs and falcons. He gambled at cards, chess and dice, often losing large sums of money. During holidays and festivals he would pay high prices for entertainment by fools (clowns), acrobats and magicians. He supported musicians, players and whole companies of minstrels at his palaces. He patronized poets and bought many books.

The King had certain long-established sources for his income. There were revenues from the vast lands owned by the Crown— rents paid by tenant farmers on these properties. Henry's first Parliament followed a custom established earlier in the fifteenth century of granting the ruler all the duties on foreign trade collected by the customs—"tunnage and poundage," as it was known.

He raised money by another not very admirable device—conferring knighthood, the Order of the Bath, upon members of the middle class. Many did not want this honor because of the great expense connected with it. So they refused it—but for thus offending the King they had to pay him a fine.

The most profitable of these "rackets," as we might call them today, was the ancient custom of wardship. If a rich noble died, his property always went to his oldest son. But if the son was young, he became the King's ward. Until he was of age and could inherit the property, all the profits from the land went to the King.

Another profitable source of revenue came from bonds. Nobles often borrowed money from the King, but they had to sign a bond promising to repay the money in installments—always more than was actually due. And if the borrower failed to pay on time, his property could be seized by the King. Thus the King was a "loan shark" of his time.

All fines levied against people who broke the law were supposed to go to the King. Before Henry VII came to the throne, collecting these revenues was controlled by the Exchequer. Surprisingly little of it reached the King, and a great deal seemed to stick to the fingers of those who collected the fines.

Henry changed all this. Rulers of England had long had their councils of nobles, who advised the sovereign on matters of government. Henry's Council was unusually large, but it appears that the real power was centered in a sort of inner council, consisting of nobles the King trusted fully and considered able men.

Using this powerful inner council, Henry was able to change

the system under which most of the government's revenues went into the Exchequer. Gradually, most of this money was diverted into the King's own coffers and the chief of the Exchequer, the Treasurer, became little more than a figurehead.

Henry VII then did something about the fines collected which never reached the King. He sent two members of his inner council, Richard Empson and Edmund Dudley, to travel about the kingdom and investigate. They did such a thorough job that the privy purse became fat indeed. They put the fear of royal vengeance into the hearts of the tax collectors, and as a result Empson and Dudley became two of the most hated men in England. Few people realized that they were merely puppets, with King Henry behind the scenes pulling the strings that controlled the two councillors' actions.

Except for his brief tussle with King James IV of Scotland and one rather ill-considered invasion of France that did not last long, Henry kept England out of foreign wars all through his reign. This saved a great deal of money, enabled England to trade freely with other countries and increased prosperity in the kingdom by developing manufactures, especially the valuable woolen cloth trade.

When Henry sent Empson and Dudley out on their missions, it was also part of his effort to restore law and order to England, for the two commissioners were able to watch and sometimes catch those who were defrauding the King.

Henry was also using other means to restore justice. He put a law through Parliament in 1487 that gave an already existing court real power. It became famous—and later infamous—as the Star Chamber, because it is supposed to have met in a room in Westminster where the walls and ceiling were ornamented with stars. It became infamous in later reigns because its great powers were used for tyrannical purposes, but in Henry's VII's time it was most valuable.

The system of justice in England when Henry's reign began was in terrible condition. Nobles and other rich men could buy themselves free from almost any crime. The Star Chamber, made up of several Council members, did have tyrannical powers, but it could strike at the most powerful lords in England who had done wrong and see that they were punished.

Today, such a court would never be permitted in either Britain or the United States. The judges, selected with great care by the King so that they could not be bribed, had tremendous power. They alone decided guilt or innocence and dealt out punishment, for there were no juries in the Court of Star Chamber. They could make a man confess under torture and sentence him to any punishment except death. It was not true justice, but it was the best way in those days to stop corruption and lawlessness among nobles and officials.

Conditions in the lower courts were shameful all over England. The all-powerful men in these courts were justices of the peace. Today, in the United States, justices of the peace are minor officials in villages, much like the magistrates and police court judges in larger places. But in England in Henry VII's time, a justice of the peace was a man to be greatly feared.

A justice of the peace conducted trials, including criminal cases of all kinds except those for treason. He had authority to order jurors to investigate everything from disturbing the peace, selling things at exorbitant prices and using false weights and measures up to the most serious crimes, called felonies. He could regulate wages. These and many more duties were the responsibilities of a justice of the peace.

He was no common man. In an English county—or shire, as

35

it is also called—there would be a number of them, depending upon the size and population of the shire. Leading the list would usually be the county's bishop. Then would come nobles and other rich landowners, followed by professional judges and high-ranking lawyers, and finally a large group of knights and squires who did most of the hard work connected with the job.

Next in power came the sheriff. He had long been an important official. Robin Hood, the benevolent outlaw, robbed the rich to help the poor, and was always outwitting the sheriff of Nottingham, who wanted to catch Robin and his Merry Men and hang them. Although Robin Hood is a legendary figure, it appears that he may have lived in the twelfth and thirteenth centuries. Thus, even some three hundred years before Henry VII's time, the sheriff was a feared and mighty man.

The sheriff arrested accused persons, summoned defendants to court, selected jurors for all court cases, seized property when decrees for this were issued, collected all Crown revenues in the county, kept accounts of these collections and made arrangements for elections of members of Parliament.

A corrupt county official could make a great deal of money for himself. The sheriffs were the worst, and the hardest to catch. A corrupt one might easily be bribed not to locate an accused wrongdoer and arrest him. In selecting jurors, he could pick those he knew would favor a person who had paid him a bribe and was on trial or was implicated in a dispute brought to court. And since he collected the Crown revenues in the shire, it was often easy for him to let some of the money stay in his own pocket and falsify his accounts.

Henry VII was well aware of these corrupt sheriffs. One weapon he used against them was to haul suspected ones before the Star Chamber, and there are a number of records of this being done. The corrupt sheriff could not bribe the Star Chamber's members to find him innocent as he might do in a shire court, and fear of severe punishment helped to keep many a sheriff honest. Justices of the peace were also able to collect bribes and cheat true justice, but Henry was able to control this quite well by being careful to select men he felt he could trust in these high offices.

However, the best means of improving justice in the counties and keeping the officials there honest was through those two royal bloodhounds, Empson and Dudley. They traveled all over England, and no one knew when they might suddenly appear and demand to see all records and accounts.

Henry also appointed Edward Belknap to a new position, Surveyor of the King's Prerogative. Belknap and a force of assistants went into eighteen counties where it was especially hard to collect the King's revenues. They were not paid salaries, but they received a generous share of the fines they imposed upon those they sought out who had not paid. As a result, Belknap and his surveyors did such a thorough job that both they and the King profited greatly, though like Empson and Dudley they were detested, while Henry escaped the people's wrath.

Nevertheless, there was a real crime wave in England, and King Henry went after criminals by allowing the justices of the peace to punish offenders themselves, except in serious crimes, without using jurors. Also, if a justice of the peace suspected that a juror had been bribed, he could remove the man or replace him.

Henry also managed to curb to some extent a notorious way of evading punishment for almost any crime. Since the twelfth century, clergymen convicted of crimes had not been executed or sent to prison. Instead, they were handed over to the nearest bishop, who generally let them off by imposing some sort of penance. By the late Middle Ages this "benefit of clergy" had been extended to all those who could read, since few but clergymen could, anyway.

Suddenly, however, learning to read became of great importance in England. By the middle of the fifteenth century, so many criminals went free because they had learned to read a little that the government tried to put an end to benefit of clergy except to real clergymen, but these efforts failed.

[Henry VII tried again with more success. In 1489 he got Parliament to pass a new law, under which a convicted layman who pleaded benefit of clergy was allowed to go free once. But he was branded on the thumb to show that he had escaped punishment. If he committed a second crime, he could not get off by such a plea.]

Another way in which criminals evaded arrest was by escaping to sanctuary. An offender could go into any church and remain there forty days without being arrested, and at the end of that time he did not have to go to prison or be executed, but was simply banished from England. There were also a number of "great sanctuaries," among them Westminster Abbey. If a criminal could reach one of these, he was safe as long as he wanted to stay there.

Henry VII could not do much about these great sanctuaries without offending the powerful Church. But he was able to make them unpopular for those who went into them to escape imprisonment for debt. Many of these debtors were well able to pay out of the incomes from their property. To avoid seizure of these lands to pay their debts, they simply transferred their ownership to trusted friends, who paid them the income so that they could live comfortably in sanctuary. Henry got Parliament

38

to pass a law forbidding such transfers of property. After that, more people paid their bills.

The King's government was more democratic than ever before, since more men of the middle class were becoming wealthy and influential enough to win seats in the House of Commons of Parliament. Actually, however, because Henry VII's talent as an administrator enabled him to restore England to peace, better justice and greater prosperity, during the first twelve years of his reign he had to call only six Parliaments; in the last twelve he called only one.

Henry VII never fully controlled the lawless distant borders of his kingdom, including wild, mountainous and rebellious Wales, even though he himself was a Welshman. And no English ruler before Henry had been able to subdue Ireland, except for Dublin; but he had better luck, though not to the advantage of the oppressed Irish people.

In 1494 Henry sent Sir Edward Poynings to Ireland as Lord Deputy, or governor. Poynings was a strong man who managed to bring the Irish Parliament under his control and pass several acts known as the "Poynings Laws." One provided that the Irish Parliament could make no laws without the King's consent; another that all laws passed by the English Parliament should apply to Ireland.

For centuries the Poynings Laws destroyed all hope of real freedom for the Irish. But Henry VII was smart enough to head off the serious rebellion that might have resulted. He recalled Poynings and sent the Earl of Kildare, a former governor, back to Ireland as Lord Deputy again. Kildare was an Irishman, born Gerald Fitzgerald, popular with the Irish people yet loyal to the King and an able Lord Deputy. He gave Henry VII what he wanted—no serious rebellion against England in Ireland.

England's increasing prosperity during Henry VII's reign was due mainly, of course, to the growth of the wool and cloth trade. But Henry negotiated treaties that opened new markets in Spain and France, permitted English trade in the Mediterranean for the first time, with Italy and Greece, and also with Iceland, and enabled England to keep its share of the profitable trade with the Low Countries, just across the North Sea.

Bigger ships were being built under Henry's encouragement, since they could be used by the navy in case of war. He also constructed warships of his own. One, the *Regent*, was 700 tuns (the old word for tons), a monster for those days, and carried 225 cannon. Also, for the first time, some of her big guns were mounted below the top deck and could be fired all at once in deadly broadsides through portholes called gunports.

Always on the lookout for new markets for English sea trade, Henry pricked up his ears when he heard about John Cabot. Cabot was a Venetian seafaring man whose real name was Giovanni Caboto, but its English spelling was used when he settled in the English seaport of Bristol. His great ambition was to find a sea passage to the rich lands of China and Japan.

Henry VII knew about the fabulous products of the Far East —spices, silks and other valuable products—which then reached Europe only by the long and dangerous journey over land. When the news reached England that Christopher Columbus, backed by Spain, had discovered a sea route to what was thought to be a part of the Far East, Henry issued letters patent giving Cabot and his three sons the sole right to make voyages of discovery for the benefit of England.

The Cabots sailed from Bristol in a tiny ship in 1497. They are supposed to have done what Columbus had failed to do—

land directly on the continent of North America in Newfoundland.

[Another benefit for England in Henry VII's reign was the care he took to keep on good terms with the Roman Catholic Church, the only one then allowed in England, and with its powerful popes. The Church was very rich, and Henry supported it strongly. Others were generous too; almost everyone with money left bequests to the Church in his will.]

/ Meanwhile, on September 19, 1486, just a little over a year after the victory of Bosworth Field put Henry Tudor on the throne, his wife, Queen Elizabeth, gave birth to a son, who was named Arthur. Of course, there was great rejoicing and celebration all over England, for now the first Tudor ruler had an heir to succeed him. /

Arthur's parents had great plans for him. After long negotiations, his marriage to Princess Catherine of Aragon, daughter of Christopher Columbus' famous patrons, King Ferdinand and Queen Isabella of powerful Spain, was arranged in 1496. Arthur was then only ten years old and his bride-to-be about a year younger, but royal marriages were usually arranged in this way, sometimes when the two children were no more than babies. They were not married until 1501, when Arthur was fifteen and Catherine fourteen.

/ As the sixteenth century began, Henry VII was becoming old as lifetimes went in those days, although in 1500 he was only forty-three. For some years his health had not been good. In 1501 he is described as having a drawn face, with the skin over his jaws bluish and his temples hollow, though his eyes had lost none of their keen, foxy and alert look. In 1503 he had a case of quinsy, an inflammation of the tonsils, which was so severe that for six days he could neither eat nor drink. |

From then on, his health declined and some of his bad traits increased. Always suspicious of everything and everybody, he became more so. His craftiness, greed and meanness showed more plainly.

At last, on April 22, 1509, Henry VII, the first of the Tudor rulers, died at his well-loved palace of Richmond. Of all the Tudors except perhaps the boy King Edward VI, he is probably the least remembered, but one of the best of them, if not *the* best. Yet he did leave one living although not important reminder of his reign that still exists today—the famous Beefeaters.

Naturally, a great fortress-palace-prison like the Tower of London has had guards ever since William the Conqueror built it in the eleventh century. It remained for Henry VII, who loved splendor and show so much, to establish a new corps called the Yeomen of the Guard. He put them into red tunics trimmed with purple and gold, red knee breeches and stockings, a ruff around their necks and plumed hats, and they carried the medieval half-lance and the half-ax called the halberd, as well as a sword. The Beefeaters, as everyone calls them, look almost exactly the same today as they guard not only the Tower, but also the sovereign of Britain.

Henry also began the custom of addressing the sovereign as "your Majesty." However, "your Grace," the previous form, was also used for some time. "Your Majesty" was part of Henry's plan that changed England so much—to make people realize the power and majesty of the Crown, while taking away much of the great lords' power and making it possible for the common people to have a strong voice in the government and gain some of the wealth that had formerly been held almost entirely by the nobility. This was the greatest of all his accomplishments.

42

4

The King of Many Faces...

NO ONE CAN DENY THAT HENRY VIII is one of the most famous of all English rulers. Probably more people know about him than any other king England ever had. His reign was a strange combination of good and evil. Unfortunately, the evil things outnumbered the good. Also, many of the events of his reign that changed the course of English history were carried out mainly by Henry's chief ministers, especially Thomas, Cardinal Wolsey, and by Thomas Cromwell, so Henry can seldom claim full credit even for the good actions.

Henry VIII himself was the perfect image of a king—handsome, burly, strong, vigorous. In general, the common people among his subjects loved and almost worshiped "bluff King Hal," as they called him, and for the most part forgave him his faults, sins and cruelties. A very famous king, yes, but scarcely a good man.

Cruel he certainly could be, and often was, yet he could be merciful, tender and forgiving. But to his enemies or those who offended or failed him, he was as dangerous as a coiled cobra.

Always, Henry VIII had to have his own way. He would listen to counsel and give great authority to those he considered trustworthy and competent; but what Henry wanted, Henry must have. In one way or another he swept away those who opposed him. He never lost control of his Parliaments, and thus he never had the trouble with them that other rulers had.

At the time of Henry's birth, no one expected him to become King of England. His brother Arthur, five years older, was the heir to the throne and, as far as anyone knew then, perfectly healthy. Naturally, as a prince of the royal blood, Henry was carefully brought up and educated, but the training for kingship went to Arthur.

Nevertheless, Henry received many honors while he was little more than a baby. By this English custom of conferring honors so early, before he was four years old Henry held the important posts of Constable of Dover Castle and Warden of the Cinque Ports, Earl Marshall of England, Lieutenant (or governor) of Ireland, Warden of the northern borders of England called the Scottish Marches and Duke of York. Adult noblemen carried out the duties of these positions for him. He was also a knight of the distinguished orders of the Bath and the Garter.

His education was chiefly in the classic books of the great Greek and Roman writers, and in modern languages and music, which he always loved. Whether Henry liked his first tutor, John Skelton, the poet laureate of England, is doubtful. Skelton had a sharp tongue and seems not to have been afraid to use it on a royal prince. He demanded nothing less than perfection from his pupil and wrote a handbook of advice for Henry. The prince, however, showed a flash of what was to come; even then he was not fond of being told what to do, and paid no attention at all to the handbook.

By the time Henry was ten, he was big and tall for his age, a handsome boy with red-gold hair, fair complexion and a round face. He bore little resemblance to the King he was to be. This angelic-looking child would grow to be a hulking, bearded giant with an imperious, demanding presence and eyes that could make those in high places cower before their penetrating gaze. Yet he could be demanding and willful even then.

At the age of ten, Henry enjoyed one of the great times of his childhood. Prince Arthur's bride-to-be, Catherine of Aragon, arrived in London. Since she was allowed to see little of Arthur before the wedding, was shy and spoke no English, Henry gallantly took it upon himself to be her escort.

He took Catherine about the city, mounted on a splendid horse, while she trotted beside him on a mule. The crowds cheered this Spanish princess, no great beauty but handsome and regal in her Spanish-style clothes and wide-brimmed hat, worn at a jaunty angle over her auburn hair. Henry bore himself proudly, feeling that the people's enthusiasm included admiration of himself, second son of Henry VII and Duke of York, the highest title in the realm below that of the King and of Arthur, Prince of Wales.

Proudly too, he headed the wedding procession from Baynard's Castle to St. Paul's, and led the bride into the cathedral. After the ceremony came days of festivities and the bridal couple's retirement to the royal castle at Ludlow in the west country. But Prince Arthur was already racked by a cough no medicine could stop. Four months later he died.

Henry, not yet eleven, was heir to the throne. About a year later he was given his brother's title of Prince of Wales. But when he was officially betrothed to Arthur's widow, Catherine of Aragon, who was six years older, Henry VII was inclined to agree when his son said he did not want to marry her. Catherine's mother, famous Queen Isabella, the actual ruler of Spain, had died. Thus her husband, Ferdinand, was no longer called Spain's King, but only King of Aragon, then a separate kingdom, not nearly so powerful or rich. Henry's father decided he could find a better bride for his son, especially since the 100,000 crowns of Catherine's enormous dowry she was to bring Arthur was still unpaid.

It was the beginning of years of misery and unhappiness for Prince Arthur's young widow. Nothing was done about the expected marriage to Prince Henry. They put Catherine in Durham House, a not very palatial medieval mansion on the banks of the Thames, almost a prisoner.

Catherine wanted very much to marry young Henry. She wrote passionate appeals to her father to do something about the dowry. He paid no attention. When she occasionally saw the King, Henry VII did nothing but complain.

"Why does his Highness not keep his word and pay the dowry?" the King would demand. "It is only our goodwill that makes us give you food to eat. You have no claim on us."

They did not give her a great deal to eat, much less proper clothing. One of her piteous letters to her father tells how she sold some bracelets to buy a black velvet dress, since she had almost nothing to wear. She was not allowed to see Prince Henry at all.

In 1509 Catherine's marriage troubles suddenly ended, though there was only unhappiness in her future. Less than two months after King Henry VII's death, the new King married her. Why Henry VIII did so is something of a mystery, although he claimed it was his father's dying wish. There is no indication that he ever loved her, yet Catherine was a fine woman—attractive enough, intelligent and cultured—though, of course, too old for Henry.

The new King had to be crowned. No expense was spared to make it the greatest spectacle London had ever seen. On June 23, 1509, Henry and his Queen rode in a procession from the Tower of London through the City to the palace at Westminster.

Practically every inhabitant who could walk, and thousands from the surrounding countryside, were jammed along the sides of the route from the Tower through Gracechurch Street, along broad, shop-lined Cheapside, through the arched gateway of Temple Bar and down the Strand to Westminster. These streets were hung with rich tapestries and cloth of gold. The cheering populace craned their necks to catch a glimpse of Henry, in crimson robes trimmed with ermine, and Catherine, in white satin, under their canopies. Henry fairly radiated fire of many colors—the flash of such a great number of precious stones that they all but hid his royal attire.

The next day the royal pair went from the palace to nearby Westminster Abbey. A cloth carpet paved the route, which the crowd tore to ribbons for souvenirs after Henry and Catherine had entered the Abbey.

Inside, Henry went through the ancient rite of coronation. He was shown to the people squeezed into every inch of the Abbey by the Archbishop of Canterbury, who asked four times if they accepted him as their sovereign, and four times a roar went up: "God save King Henry!"

The King then took the oath of office and prostrated himself before the altar while his robes were drawn aside so that he could be anointed with the holy oil used only at coronations. At last the Imperial Crown was placed upon his head. Now indeed, Henry VIII was King of England, France (England, though holding only the tiny wedge of France around Calais, still claimed it all) and Ireland.

Afterwards, an unbelievably lavish banquet was held in Westminster Hall, which like Westminster Abbey still stands today. The dinner was said to be "greater than any Caesar had known" in the extravagant days of his rule of the vast Roman Empire. The Duke of Buckingham and the Lord Steward clip-clopped into the hall on horseback, leading a long line of servants bearing meats and delicacies of every sort, with which the invited guests stuffed themselves while they drank the finest wines.

That was only the beginning. After the meal a great tournament was held in which knights jousted until nightfall. There followed days of revelry, feasting, dancing, singing, pageants, more jousting and tilting and hunting and hawking.

The one central figure of all this was King Henry VIII. Queen Catherine was crowned with him, but she was overshadowed by her lusty, brawny, uproarious, gem-studded husband, whose subjects were sure that here was England's greatest king.

Indeed, in the months that followed, Henry VIII seems to have had interests more important to him than romantic life with his bride and Queen. He was tall, a magnificent figure with his gleaming hair and fair, creamy complexion. An expert horseman, he loved to spend hours in the saddle hunting or hawking (in which falcons were trained to swoop down on birds, rabbits and other small game with their cruel, sharp beaks and talons). Henry liked to wrestle, dance, play tennis and engage in mock combat with nobles of his Court with great, two-handed swords. He could throw a spear straight to a target many yards away, and rival the fabled Robin Hood at drawing a huge, taut-stringed bow and sending an arrow whizzing to the mark.

Henry's subjects marveled at all of this, and at the tales of his luxurious way of living—his reckless gambling, the jeweled rings that crammed his fingers, the golden collar set with a walnut-size diamond, the other flashing gems that trimmed the cloth of gold, silk, satin, velvet and feathers he wore. They loved him— and as long as they behaved and obeyed him, Henry VIII loved his people too.

They gave little thought to where the money to pay for all this came from or would come from in the future—their own pockets. If, as some said, the privy purse was bulging when Henry VII died, Henry VIII would drain it—the quicker, the better. And once the purse was empty, Henry VIII did not worry about re-filling it. His father had put England on a sound financial basis; but for the ways his son would find to amass new riches, Henry VIII would have bankrupted the kingdom.

Henry pleased his subjects by one act soon after he came to the throne. His father's hated tax collectors, Empson and Dudley, were brought to trial, convicted and beheaded. They were actually innocent victims of Henry VII's orders, but the people rejoiced at their fate.

The actual governing of England was the last thing Henry wanted to be bothered with. He had to know and approve everything that was done, but the doing was left to his ministers, especially the chief one—Thomas, Cardinal Wolsey, a curious mixture of good and evil, of the greatest intelligence and ability, arrogant, domineering, rude, immensely rich, treacherous and wily.

Wolsey was born in 1472 or 1473 in Ipswich, Suffolk, the son of a butcher. He is another illustration of how, from the time of Henry VII on, a boy from a humble family could rise high.

Thomas Wolsey went to Magdalen College at Oxford University. He was so brilliant that he became known as the "boy bachelor," because he attained his bachelor of arts degree before he was fifteen. He was appointed to a post in the college, became its bursar, or treasurer, and in 1498 was ordained a priest.

But a little later Wolsey seems to have shown signs of what he was to become—as imperious and self-willed a man as Henry VIII himself. According to legend, Wolsey decided that Magdalen College should have the handsomest tower of the whole university. So he laid out the money to build the tower, apparently without consulting his superiors about it.

Beautiful it was and is today—the pride of all Oxford's buildings, an architectural gem that ranks with the finest in all England. But the authorities did not like such high-handed ways and, so the story goes, asked Wolsey to resign.

This did not end his troubles. The Marquis of Dorset took the young man under his wing and had him installed as the priest of a church in a small Somerset village. But Wolsey, who liked a good time, seems to have had too much ale at a country fair. He insulted a man who turned out to be a justice of the peace and put Wolsey in the stocks. This was a sort of panel set on a scaffold in a public place. The offender's arms and legs were locked into holes in the stocks, a great temptation not only to mischievous boys but also to older people, to pelt the culprit with rotten eggs and fruit, and abuse.

Wolsey could not be stopped by such a disgrace. He managed to worm his way into the royal Court. By 1507 he was chaplain to Henry VII. Not long after the death of the first Tudor king, Henry VIII appointed him royal almoner, in charge of giving alms and charity to the poor, and also a royal councillor.

From then on, Wolsey's influence over King Henry VIII grew steadily. Henry saw that here was a man who was an able administrator who could be most useful. Wolsey knew how to cut red tape and get things done. Stepping on the toes of those above him in the government did not bother him at all.

Wolsey's rise was meteoric. Within three years after Henry VIII's coronation he was the King's private war minister; in 1514 he became Archbishop of York, the second highest prelate in England. The following year Pope Leo X made him a cardinal, and Henry VIII appointed him first Lord Chancellor and then Prime Minister of England. He now occupied the highest positions in the realm under the King. Being a prelate did not keep him from holding high government office, since churchmen of high rank often did.

For twenty years Wolsey used the tremendous power Henry VIII had given him and kept the King satisfied and not even suspicious that the cardinal often used power that belonged to the King. Wolsey's ambition was boundless. He made the most of his power. One of his biographers called him "the haughtiest man alive." He was an autocrat and a tyrant, yet with keen wit and affability he could beguile anyone he thought would be useful to him. On the other hand, he could be outrageously bad-mannered to his inferiors.

Wolsey lived in the grandest and most extravagant style. He usually resided in his magnificent palace of More outside London, and when he tired of it there were three others he had built. A fourth, Hampton Court, still standing today, he gave to the King when Henry VIII admired it, and it became Henry's favorite palace.

Wolsey got back what this gift had cost, and more. Between 1513 and 1529 his yearly income was estimated at £9,500. By modern money values this would be about a quarter of a million dollars a year. By 1531 his income is believed to have risen to £35,000 a year, close to a million dollars today.

How did he get it? Not as Prime Minister and Chancellor. Because of his power and his cardinal's red hat, he was able to obtain a former bishop's property and possessions when a vacancy for the bishop's seat occurred. And in all the foreign treaties Wolsey negotiated for the King, he saw to it that he was "rewarded" with a few thousand pounds, in one way or another.

Wolsey's portrait gives few clues to the man behind the face. It does show a small, hard mouth, large, cold, calculating eyes and the look of a man who will get what he wants by fair means or foul.

Wolsey's robes were of the richest materials. The household servants in his palaces were figured at 429 in 1526; at the same time, Henry VIII's daughter, the Princess Mary, had only sixty-five. The cardinal's official household included one earl, nine barons and about a thousand knights, gentlemen and lower officials. He dined sumptuously, though he did limit himself to nine dishes a meal, perhaps to keep from becoming as fat as a hog ready for slaughter.

Unfortunately, in spite of Wolsey's genius, Henry VIII put too much trust in him a few years after he came to the throne. Henry had decided that he would be a warrior king, invade France and gain back all the territory that had been lost.

England joined the Holy League, started by Pope Julius II. It included Venice, Spain and the Holy Roman Empire, which took in most of what is now Germany. The plan was to overwhelm France.

England declared war on France in 1512 and sent two large armies to join the others of the League. But these allies failed to support them and made peace with France. The English campaign was a miserable failure.

But now Henry VIII had Wolsey to help him. In 1513 there was another English invasion of France. Henry himself led the army and this time had a little more success. The English had captured the French city of Tournai, but Wolsey gave it back in exchange for a pension for himself of 12,000 French francs a year, along with a large payment to Henry VIII from King Francis I of France. He also arranged for a marriage between Henry's infant daughter Mary and Francis' son, the Dauphin, or heir to the French throne, who was also a baby. Wolsey's crowning achievement was in setting up a meeting between Henry VIII and Francis I in France. It was to be a love feast that would establish peace between the two countries.

This meeting was carried out with such magnificence that it is celebrated in history as the Field of the Cloth of Gold. Henry and Queen Catherine went to France in 1520, taking with them five thousand persons, including practically all the nobility of

England, along with tons of fine clothing, food and dishes, jewels of untold value and hundreds of tents and pavilions. Six thousand laborers worked to practically rebuild the palace of Guines near Calais and erect a gorgeous summer palace near it that looked like a castle out of a fairy tale.

On June 7, 1520, on the Field of the Cloth of Gold, the two kings met in unbelievable pomp and splendor. They embraced each other and held a conference, pledging eternal friendship between the two nations. Wolsey, in all his glory, sang a solemn High Mass and preached a sermon on peace.

Actually, the whole great spectacle meant nothing. During the festivities that followed the meeting, Francis I threw Henry VIII in a wrestling match. The burly Henry prided himself on being invincible in this sport, and the French King's triumph had at least some influence in soon setting the two countries at each other's throats again.

In 1521 war broke out between France and Spain. Henry VIII sent Wolsey to Paris to try to negotiate peace between the warring countries, but Wolsey had other plans to achieve the greatest ambition of his life. He wanted to become Pope and be the first Englishman ever to sit on the throne of St. Peter's in Rome.

Wolsey decided that the Holy Roman Emperor, Charles V, who was also King of Spain, was the man who could make him Pope once Pope Leo X died. Charles V agreed to do so in exchange for a secret alliance with England. Wolsey arranged the treaty while he continued to pretend friendship for Francis I of France. Pope Leo soon obliged Wolsey by dying, but Charles V double-crossed the cardinal by getting one of his own favorites elected as Pope Adrian VI.

Nevertheless, Wolsey soon forgave Charles V and decided that England should join Spain in a new war on France. It was to be a mighty effort that would cost an enormous amount of money to prepare for and fight.

Wolsey came back to England and set about raising it. Most of the money came from the well-known system of forced loans, whereby rich nobles and merchants were "requested" to lend the King money they dared not refuse.

Even that was not enough. Wolsey got Henry VIII to summon a Parliament in 1523 to pass a backbreaking tax of four shillings for each pound of value of everyone's land, other possessions and money to raise £800,000. There was a small war over it in Parliament, which finally granted part of Wolsey's demands.

Two English armies were sent to France, but the campaign seemed doomed to failure, largely because it cost far more than Wolsey had estimated. Meanwhile, Adrian VI died in December, 1523, after a short reign. Again Charles V promised to help Wolsey succeed Adrian, and again played him false. Pope Clement VII came to the throne of St. Peter.

This time Wolsey struck back. The English army had managed to come within thirty miles of Paris that winter, ready to strike and capture the capital. Then, suddenly, the soldiers were withdrawn by the cardinal's order. It was vengeance upon Charles V, but Wolsey glibly explained it to Henry VIII by telling of the bitter cold and the many soldiers who had frozen to death. England, through Wolsey, then made peace and an alliance with France.

Meanwhile, Charles V won an overwhelming victory over the French and became master of the Continent of Europe. But Wolsey still hoped to beat him. In 1525 he got the royal Council to demand one-sixth of every Englishman's wealth and possessions to carry on the war.

The English people were infuriated. They cursed this money-mad cardinal who was trying to ruin them. A rebellion broke out in Suffolk. At last Henry VIII stepped in and withdrew the demand.

Wolsey had gone too far. Henry VIII himself began to suffer from the cardinal's scheming. With the wars costing so much, the King was running short of cash for his own living expenses. He started issuing gold and silver coins that did not have the proper amount of the precious metal in them. Debasing the currency in this way caused inflation and damaged England's prosperity.

Meanwhile, something else was going on that would have an even more serious effect on England's future. On New Year's Day, 1511, Queen Catherine had given birth to a son named Henry. His father, Henry VIII, was delirious with joy. He had what he wanted most of all—a son to succeed him. But seven weeks later the child died.

The couple had one daughter, Mary, but Henry wanted a son. Catherine was now getting too old to have more children. Besides, Henry had long since grown tired of devoted, loyal Catherine of Aragon. There were dozens of lovely ladies in the Court who would have sold their souls to Satan for a romance with the King. In fact, some did have it without selling their souls. But Henry wanted a wife of proper rank who would give him another son and heir.

Then Anne Boleyn, who had been in France as one of the royal household of Francis I's Queen, returned home to England in 1522 and entered the Court there. Henry VIII's eye softened the first time it fell upon the nineteen-year-old Anne. She was not a ravishing beauty, but her Irish ancestors had given her hair a dark glory; she had lovely dark eyes and a sparkling, vivacious personality that quickly bewitched the King.

Henry soon fell madly in love with Anne Boleyn. He had to have her for his wife. But how to get rid of Catherine of Aragon? An annulment of the marriage or a divorce would have to be obtained from the Pope. And who was better qualified to handle this than Wolsey?

In May, 1527, the King sent for the cardinal and told him what he had to do. Wolsey was stunned. He feared that the end of Henry's marriage to Catherine would cause untold trouble for England in Catholic Europe, especially Spain. He fell to his knees and with tears running down his face implored Henry to forget this foolish dream.

His words bounced off the King like rubber balls off a brick wall. In back of that wall stood Anne Boleyn. She did not like Wolsey. She had worked on the King to make sure he would not listen to the objections she knew the cardinal would have. From then on it was war to the death between them—to Wolsey's death, at least.

"You will see Warham about this, my Lord Chancellor," the King declared. "Together you must arrange matters so that my marriage to the Lady Anne Boleyn may take place."

"I will do as you command, your Majesty," Wolsey mumbled. He kissed the King's hand and withdrew.

5

Wolsey, Anne Boleyn and the Break With Rome

AS ORDERED, WOLSEY MET WITH William Warham, Archbishop of Canterbury, the highest prelate of England. Warham did not object to the plan. He had never favored the marriage to Catherine of Aragon, anyway, and he wanted to keep the King's favor. Wolsey, too, knew that he would have to go along with the King's desire.

Rome's approval had to be gained. Otherwise, if Henry and Anne married without it and had a son, he would be illegitimate and his inheritance of the throne endangered.

The two prelates decided that Henry's marriage to Catherine would be declared illegal by a court of the highest authority, and the Pope's approval then sought. The basis for the court's decision would be the biblical law in the Book of Leviticus forbidding a man to marry his brother's wife, as Henry had married Prince Arthur's widow.

Meanwhile, this plan became extremely complicated. On May 5, 1527, a Spanish army burst into Rome and sacked the city. In the Vatican, the new Pope, Clement VII, and his attendants scurried by a secret passage to the nearby ancient circular stone fortress of the Castel Sant' Angelo. There Clement was safe from the ferocious Spaniards, but still the prisoner of Charles V. And Charles was Catherine of Aragon's nephew. How would the Pope dare grant Henry VIII's demands now?

On June 22, 1527, Henry faced Catherine with the news that their marriage was to be ended.

"We have been living in mortal sin, since you were my brother's wife," he told her. "You must retire from the Court until our marriage is dissolved."

Catherine burst into tears. At last, controlling herself, she said with calm dignity and great firmness, "I will not agree to this. I am prepared to meet any argument for our separation."

Henry had expected no resistance. He stared at her, dumfounded. Then he said, "I pray you, keep this a secret," and withdrew.

In Charles V's assault on Rome, Wolsey's agile mind saw a solution to the difficulty. He set off for France to meet a group of cardinals at Avignon. He would persuade them to grant him Clement VII's authority while the Pope was a prisoner. Thus he himself could dissolve Henry's marriage to Catherine, and Anne Boleyn would become the new Queen.

But Henry VIII and Anne Boleyn secretly sent Henry's secretary, William Knight, to Rome to obtain the Pope's signature to a document ending the King's marriage to Catherine. In France, Wolsey learned of the mission. He was stunned and grievously hurt. For the first time, as far as he knew, the King had deceived him. Worse, Henry had sent a man to Rome who knew nothing of the arts of diplomacy.

Wolsey set off for England at once to plead with Henry to

recall Knight. But when he tried to obtain an audience with the King, he was told Henry was with Anne Boleyn and would see the cardinal only if Anne approved. Wolsey began to see his power slipping.

Wolsey was right. Lacking the cardinal's skill and experience with diplomacy and delicate intrigue, Knight botched his errand. He came back with a signed document, all right—a papal bull, as it is called—but it was worthless unless Henry could furnish proof acceptable to the Pope that his marriage to Catherine was illegal. Clement VII was not a strong man, and he had reasons for evading a decision about the marriage.

There followed endless negotiations. Wolsey tried to save the situation—and his own future—by sending three experienced envoys to Rome. But Clement only dodged by issuing more worthless bulls.

Meanwhile, Catherine herself was fighting desperately to save her marriage. The King sent a representative to Catherine to frighten her by threats into retiring to a nunnery. She was so popular with the people that Henry wanted her out of the way lest his subjects rebel and force him to give up his plans.

But Catherine would not be intimidated. With that, Henry moved her from the palace at Richmond to Hampton Court, and Anne Boleyn took over her apartments next to the King's. He and Anne were now living together as if they had been married, Pope or no Pope.

Finally the court Wolsey and the Archbishop of Canterbury had set up met and heard Catherine of Aragon present her story. Three days later both she and Henry appeared before the judges. There was a pitiful scene when Catherine knelt and implored her husband not to cast her out. Afterwards, she sent an appeal to the Pope, who replied by sending an order to England dissolving the court.

Henry VIII was enraged. Like a spoiled child, he looked around for someone besides himself to take the blame. He decided that Wolsey should be the scapegoat.

Among Wolsey's bitter enemies, the Dukes of Suffolk and Norfolk were the bitterest. They formed a party to take advantage of the King's wrath and topple the cardinal from power.

A little later, for a time, it seemed that the King had forgiven Wolsey, since he was such a valuable minister. But in August, 1529, when the cardinal was at the royal Court, then gathered at Grafton in Northamptonshire, Anne Boleyn is said to have objected to Henry's entertaining a man who had done him so much wrong. That evening, lodgings could not be found for Wolsey, who had to ride a mule three miles through the darkness to an inn.

Wolsey's enemies drew up forty-four charges against him. It was said that he had injured the liberties of Church and Crown, accused clergy of unmentionable offenses, robbed religious houses, embezzled the goods of bishops whose vacant seats he had taken over, made unauthorized treaties, taken equal authority to that of the King, made the poor suffer from unjust taxes and fines and been greedy and extravagant, accepting bribes and extorting money.

The Great Seal of his office as Lord Chancellor was taken from him, and he was ordered to leave his luxurious palace of York House in London for a grim, nearly empty house at Esher, a prison by comparison. Sir Thomas More replaced him as Chancellor.

It was October, 1529. Wolsey stood looking out of the window at the dreary fall landscape there at Esher. "I am like to lose all that I have worked for all the days of my life," he said sadly, "for doing of my master true and diligent service." All of the arrogance and imperiousness had gone out of him.

Early in 1530, Thomas Cromwell brought a message. "My Lord Archbishop," he said, "the Duke of Norfolk sends you word that if you do not at once leave the vicinity of the King and go north to York, he will tear you with his teeth."

"Marry, Thomas," the cardinal said, "then it is time to be doing if my Lord of Norfolk take it so."

Wolsey, still Archbishop of York, remained in that city until the late autumn. Then, one day, when he was at dinner, a troop of horsemen clattered up to his lodgings. They were led by the Duke of Northumberland.

Northumberland was pale as he laid a trembling hand on Wolsey's arm. "My Lord," he said, "I arrest you for high treason."

Through the sad November days the cardinal, aging though not old, but broken in spirit and body, rode south. On the road they met Sir William Kingston, Constable of the Tower of London, and a guard of yeomen sent to take Wolsey into custody.

Kingston tried to reassure Wolsey. "The King is friendly to you, my Lord Archbishop," he said. "He means you no harm."

Wolsey knew better. He was certain that he would be convicted of treason and sentenced to death. A pardon by the King was almost out of the question; Anne Boleyn and his other enemies were too powerful.

They reached Leicester. There, stopping at its abbey, the

cardinal, feeble and gaunt, said to his host, "Father Abbot, I am come hither to leave my bones among you."

He lived another day and a night. At eight in the morning of November 29, 1530, after confessing and being given absolution, Thomas, Cardinal Wolsey, died. He had cheated the headsman's ax, cheated Henry VIII, Anne Boleyn and his noble enemies of their prey. A greedy, evil man in many ways, who would do anything for the power he craved, he had nevertheless served the King too well to deserve his fall.

Henry's marriage to Catherine of Aragon was no nearer its end. For the first time the King struck at the Church by persuading Parliament to pass bills under which the clergy must be residents of England and could not hold more than one office in the Church under penalty of heavy fines.

Pope Clement retaliated by issuing a bull threatening to excommunicate Henry if he married Anne Boleyn. It meant that the King would go to hell when he died, and that all Catholics would be forbidden to have anything to do with him for the rest of his life.

Henry then heard something that made him prick up his ears. A priest and member of the governing body of Jesus College at Cambridge University, Thomas Cranmer, suggested that opinions on the legality of the marriage to Catherine of Aragon be obtained from learned clergy at European universities. If enough of them found it illegal, the Pope might be swayed by such wisdom.

"This fellow Cranmer has the sow by the right ear," Henry declared. "Summon him to the Court."

The priest was given a minor position in the royal household, but the King had his eye on him. Cranmer had none of Wolsey's arrogance or love of money and extravagant living. Although he was a highly intelligent scholar, he could be managed easily and was always ready to do the King's bidding. In 1532, two years after Cranmer had come to the Court, Henry appointed him Archbishop of Canterbury following Warham's death.

Of even greater importance to Henry VIII in the new government that followed Wolsey's death was Thomas Cromwell. Here was a steel trap of a man, as cold as a glacier at heart and moving as slowly and surely. Wolsey had served the King for the power and money he himself could gain. Cromwell, on the other hand, wanted to make the King more powerful and, as he once boasted, "the richest monarch in Christendom." In all his time as the King's devoted servant, Cromwell made only one mistake, and while it was actually a trivial one, it was fatal.

Thomas Cromwell was born in 1485 near London just as the first Tudor king began his reign. Here was another successful man of humble beginnings. As a boy, Thomas was hard to manage, and he either got into some kind of trouble or ran away from home. After serving as a soldier in Italy he became a merchant, first in Venice and then Amsterdam. Finally, in 1523, he returned to England, where he became both a merchant and a moneylender.

It was through his moneylending that he seems to have become acquainted with Wolsey, who often dealt with such people in obtaining loans for the King. Meanwhile, Cromwell had been studying law, became an able lawyer, began to rise under Wolsey's favor and was elected to Parliament in 1523.

Wolsey's fall did not affect Cromwell, since he stood in well with the Duke of Norfolk's party. By 1534 he was a powerful member of the Privy Council and secretary to the King.

Then there was Sir Thomas More, who succeeded Wolsey as Lord Chancellor. He was a great statesman, scholar, author and lawyer. Where character meant nothing to Cromwell, strength of character was More's greatest quality. But he never should have been named Lord Chancellor, and the King should have known better than to do so.

Cranmer's scheme for the dissolution of the King's marriage did not work, because the Pope forbade university clergy to give their opinions on it. The King then got two English archbishops, four bishops, forty noble peers and others to sign a menacing letter to Pope Clement demanding that the case be decided at once. Still the Pope delayed. Henry then tried in vain to enlist the aid of enough cardinals to depose Clement.

Suddenly, matters approached a crisis. In January, 1533, Anne Boleyn told Henry that she was going to have a child. So, in great secrecy, the King married her. In order that the child—a son, Henry hoped—might be legitimate and thus the legal heir to the throne, Archbishop Cranmer obediently declared that the King's marriage to Catherine of Aragon was null and void, and that he and Anne Boleyn were legally married. On June 1, 1533, Anne was crowned Queen of England in Westminster Abbey.

The Pope retaliated by declaring the marriage to Anne illegal and ordering them to separate. When King Henry did not obey, he was excommunicated.

On January 15, 1534, a Parliament summoned by Henry met and enacted a series of laws aimed at punishing the Catholic Church. Finally, and most important, Parliament passed the Act

65

of Supremacy. It declared that the King was "the only supreme head in earth of the Church of England."

It was the beginning of the Reformation in England, already under way in the Catholic countries of Continental Europe through the rise in power of the Protestants. It would be many years and much blood would be spilled before the Reformation in England was complete. But Henry VIII started it, and for this he is most famous.

Now that the King had what he wanted, no good came of it. Anne Boleyn had already disappointed him. On September 7, 1533, she had given birth to a daughter, Elizabeth. A girl! One can almost hear Henry VIII's snort of frustration. He had no idea, of course, that this tiny, squalling infant would become England's greatest queen.

Henry had many problems to be solved now, too. Many of the clergy were not inclined to accept the break with Rome and refused to take an oath of allegiance to Henry as supreme head of the Church of England.

One was Sir Thomas More. Henry sent him prisoner to the Tower. Another who followed More was John Fisher, Bishop of Rochester, as well as two whole cartloads of friars who had defied the King's new authority.

Meanwhile, Clement VII died and Paul III, a strong and severe man, became Pope. Since there was no way to retaliate upon Henry VIII directly, he slapped him from afar by appointing Bishop Fisher a cardinal on May 20, 1535.

Henry's rage knew no bounds. "So the Pope would put a red hat on this treasonable bishop's head!" he roared. "Forsooth, I'll send it to Rome for a fitting!"

Both Fisher and More were convicted of treason. On June 22,

the head of a prince of the Catholic Church rolled under a slash of the headsman's ax. And on July 6, Sir Thomas More went to the scaffold, not only bravely but with the best of good humor. The scaffold was so flimsily constructed that More said to the Constable of the Tower, "I pray you, Mr. Lieutenant, see me safe up, and for my coming down, let me shift for myself."

Now the King embarked on a cruel and brutal campaign to remove every trace of the Roman Catholic Church from England. His plan was to loot and then destroy every Catholic religious house in the kingdom or put it to other uses.

There were between seven and eight hundred religious houses. Many were rich and owned vast properties. Their annual income in Henry VIII's time was estimated at between £150,000 and £200,000, an incredible sum by today's values, and this did not include their gold and silver plate and other valuables.

Thomas Cromwell, now the most powerful and trusted man in Henry VIII's government, was appointed a sort of "hatchet man" to supervise the investigation of all the monasteries. Cromwell's agents spread out all over England. They ruthlessly drove some of the monastery inmates out to fend for themselves. Others were shut up, practically as prisoners, under rules so strict that many of these monks, friars, nuns and others preferred to leave also.

By an act of Parliament permitting it, the smaller monasteries with a yearly income of less than £200 suffered first. There were 327 of them, some for men, others for women of the Church. The King let fifty-two remain in return for an annual payment to him. The rest were sacked and then demolished.

Cromwell was determined to carry out his vow to make the King the richest man in Christendom. Gold from the abolished houses poured into the royal coffers as their property and valuables were sold. The property of two thousand clergymen was seized, and ten thousand farmer tenants and the servants employed in the houses found themselves deprived of their livelihood.

Especially in the north, the most strongly Catholic part of the kingdom, the people were angry and alarmed when they saw the religious houses looted and destroyed. They were devoted to their religion and relied upon it for salvation. And they believed rumors that heavy taxes were to be levied on their stock and poultry, even on baptisms, weddings and funerals. Rebellions arose.

In Lincolnshire an army of 40,000 peasants gathered, though only 16,000 had arms. But Henry sent word that he had no intention of imposing the taxes, and he also sent a strong army north. The people proved loyal, and when the King promised to pardon them if they surrendered their leaders, they did so. In March, 1537, forty-six of these leaders were executed.

Again, a force of about 34,000 who called themselves the Pilgrims of Grace rose in a religious rebellion in Yorkshire, Cumberland and Westmorland. Again Henry sent an army against them, the revolt collapsed and seventy-five men were hanged.

Parliament had decreed that the larger religious houses should be allowed to remain. Cromwell and his agents got around the law, forcing the heads of these monasteries by threats or promises of pensions and the King's favor to surrender them "voluntarily." The King got the property of all these houses, and by 1538 most of them were gone. Among the few who resisted were the abbots of Benedictine monasteries. In order to frighten the rest into submission, these abbots were given trials that were a mockery and were executed, their heads impaled on the monastery gates and parts of their quartered bodies displayed throughout the countryside.

Within three years, 188 large religious houses were abolished. True, many had grown enormously rich, largely at the expense of the poor tenant farmers on their lands and other working people, and there were evil conditions in some. And in a few cases the buildings were turned into schools and other useful projects. But the savagery with which they were despoiled and demolished left a lasting scar on England and a bitter hatred of Cromwell.

Henry's six-year effort to rid himself of Catherine of Aragon, which was ended by completely breaking with the Church of Rome in 1534, might all have been avoided if he had waited two years more. On January 8, 1536, Catherine of Aragon, still living in England, died.

Henry VIII showed his coarseness and cruelty when he heard the news. His constant worry had been that the Catholic countries of Europe might attack and try to restore Catherine to the throne.

"God be praised!" he cried. "We are delivered from all fear of war!" And he showed his joy by dressing in yellow from head to foot and joining the festivities at a ball the next day.

Yet on the very day of Catherine of Aragon's funeral, something happened that made the King begin to think he had made a mistake in marrying Anne Boleyn. For the second time during their marriage, Anne had a child who was born dead. Henry was now convinced she would never have a son, and he decided to be rid of her.

First he began to neglect her. Then, suddenly, on May 2, 1536,

69

she was arrested and sent to the Tower, charged with treason for being unfaithful to the King. It may have been true, but it was never proved.

Henry was like the Red Queen in *Alice's Adventures in Wonderland* who was always screaming, "Off with her head!" Many heads had already rolled on the orders of this ogre of a king. Now he decided to take Anne's and marry again for the son he must have.

Anne was shamefully betrayed by many people ready to testify against her. Sir Thomas Boleyn, her own father, offered to serve on the jury. Her supposed good friend, Thomas Cranmer, Archbishop of Canterbury, uttered some pious expressions of shock and grief, but this wormlike puppet of the King agreed with him that she was surely guilty. As for Thomas Cromwell, he had spied on Anne and told the King all that he saw and heard. And while she was in the Tower he sent four matrons to attend her who reported to him everything she said.

Anne was in good spirits. She did not for a moment believe the King would let her die. She ate well and she babbled—babbled too much to Cromwell's matron spies.

After two weeks in the Tower, Anne was tried by twenty-six selected peers. Her uncle, the Duke of Norfolk, presided. Anne defended herself with such a moving speech and bore herself so like a true queen that the peers were profoundly affected. Nevertheless, after hearing the evidence against her, they unanimously voted her guilty. She was sentenced to die.

Back in the Tower, Anne requested that her head be cut off by someone who could wield a sword instead of the regular headsman's ax. Since they had to send to Calais for an expert swordsman, her execution was delayed.

Anne had been hysterical after her trial, but now she was quite calm. "Master Kingston," she said to the Constable of the Tower on May 18, 1536, "I hear say that I shall not die afore noon, and I am very sorry therefor, for I had thought to be dead by this time and past my pain."

"There will be no pain," Kingston replied gently.

"I heard say the executioner was very good, and I have a little neck." She laughed merrily as she put her long, slim fingers around it.

When evening came without a summons, Anne chatted with her attendants. During the night she slept little but prayed much. She was awake at dawn when Kingston came for her.

They took her down to Tower Green. Her evil betrayer, Cromwell, was among the nobles there. Kingston assisted her up the scaffold, where stood the executioner, his assistants and the block.

She spoke in a low voice, asking forgiveness of those she had wronged and that all pray for the King, who was so good. Then she knelt and her eyes were bandaged. Twice she cried, "O God, have pity on my soul!" and had begun to repeat it a third time when the executioner's sword flashed swiftly and surely down.

So died Anne Boleyn, for whom King Henry VIII had sacrificed his country's religion. So peaceful and beautiful is Tower Green today that it is hard to believe, looking at the marker on the spot, that such bloody work went on there on May 19, 1536.

6

The Last Years

WITH REVOLTING HASTE, Henry VIII was betrothed to Jane Seymour the day after Anne Boleyn's execution, and on May 30 he married her. Jane had some royal blood, being descended on her mother's side from King Edward III. She was quiet, meek, almost prim, the exact opposite of Henry. No one considered her very beautiful, a twenty-five-year-old woman of pale complexion and medium height. She had been a lady-in-waiting to both Catherine of Aragon and Anne Boleyn.

It appears that the King began to pay her attention more than six months before Anne Boleyn's death. At first, when he wrote her letters, Jane returned them unopened. She sent back a gift of a purse of gold. Yet Jane may have been playing an artful game. For one who seemed almost prudish, it is rather curious that she would marry Henry so soon after his second queen's death. But of course, one did not disobey a command from Henry VIII.

Poor Jane Seymour—loving, loyal and gentle—had not long to be Queen of England. She had not even been crowned when,

on October 12, 1537, she gave birth to a boy, Edward. He joy was rapturous. At last he had a son to succeed him. But Seymour died twelve days after having brought little Edw into the world.

Henry VIII's grief over Jane Seymour's death was real an terrible when she was laid to rest in St. George's Chapel at Wind sor Castle. And the King did not marry again in a hurry.

Meanwhile, there were pressing matters of state to occupy him. The abolishment of the monasteries was still going on. Somehow, divided England had to be united under the new religion.

The King also wanted to extend his royal authority. Wild and lawless Wales had never really been conquered. Henry began uniting it with England by his father's system, which had worked so well in England itself—putting administration of the law under justices of the peace. Henry VIII also divided Wales into shires, which sent representatives to Parliament at Westminster. The King at least made good progress in uniting Wales with England.

Ireland, with its fiery, freedom-loving people, was a far tougher problem. After crushing a new revolt there in 1534, Henry VIII had installed a new governor, who in 1540 visited England to report that at last there was peace in Ireland. Almost immediately there was another rebellion, and since the governor had an Irish wife he was charged with treason and his head, like so many others, was lopped off. Henry then established a government in Ireland like that in Wales. It succeeded better than any other before it, and for the time being, at least, English rule was better established then ever before.

Henry was now looking for a fourth wife. He investigated several foreign ladies of high birth. The right bride from abroad

could cement friendly relations with another nation, perhaps with several, since there was so much royal intermarriage all over Europe. And Henry wanted a beautiful queen.

First he considered several royal and noble French ladies. But he had the audacity to suggest that they all be brought to English-held Calais so he could look them over. The French Court was appalled, and Henry did not become the sole judge at a beauty contest.

Henry also considered the Duchess Christina of Milan, a young widow, daughter of a former Danish king and sister of the Holy Roman Emperor, Charles V. Here was a possible marriage with great political advantages. But beautiful Christina wanted no marriage with Henry. There is a story, probably not true, that, thinking of Anne Boleyn's fate, Christina said that if she had two heads she would gladly let Henry have one of them.

Meanwhile, the King made another attempt to unify England in 1539, when Parliament enacted the Six Articles. They set forth rules for religion in England that were like those of the Roman Catholic Church. He hoped to show the people that the new religion was, after all, like their old faith. There were severe penalties for violating the Six Articles. For the first offense a person could be imprisoned and his property seized; for the second the punishment was death.

The only effect of the Six Articles was that they offended both the Protestants and the many people who clung to the old Catholic faith and believed that the Pope, not the King, was the only supreme head of the Church on earth. And Henry VIII enforced the Six Articles so harshly that they became known as the Bloody Statutes.

Henry was still looking for a fourth wife. What happened was

comical in a way, though sad for the unfortunate lady he finally chose, and fatal for powerful Thomas Cromwell.

Anne of Cleves seemed to be the leading candidate, politically. She came from an ancient German family that had important connections in Europe. Reports from those in Germany who wanted to promote the marriage said she was beautiful, but Henry had to be sure of it.

The great artist Hans Holbein was called in to do a portrait of Anne of Cleves. Perhaps the famous painter's German patriotism induced him to exaggerate a little, for the King was pleased when he saw the picture. And Thomas Cromwell, who envisioned great advantages in the marriage, praised Anne extravagantly. He had had letters from his agents abroad about her.

"Everyone praises the lady's beauty, both of face and body," he told the King. "One said she excelled the Duchess Christina as the golden sun does the silver moon." And this was the one serious mistake Thomas Cromwell ever made.

Anne of Cleves came to England. As she traveled toward London the King, in disguise, met her in Rochester. For a time only his most intimate advisers knew what he thought when he saw her. At Richmond Palace on January 3, 1540, he embraced and kissed her in public. But the truth was that Henry was appalled when he first looked at his bride-to-be. Anne was a heavily built, plain-faced German woman, thirty-four years old. She spoke not a word of English, and her only accomplishment was needlework. On the other hand, she was gentle and almost pathetically eager to please Henry.

But while the King had been so anxious not to buy "a pig in a poke"—a phrase written by an English dramatist who was also a musician at Henry VIII's Court—he had actually bought something more like an ox in a stall. What made it even worse was that because her father, the Duke of Cleves, did not have much money, the King had accepted her without a dowry.

At Rochester, Henry faced Cromwell in a fine rage. "She is nothing so well as she was spoken of," he rasped. "If I had known before as much as I know now, she should not have come within my realm." He is said to have added, "She is no better than a Flanders mare," referring to the big, clumsy Percheron draft horses of what is now Belgium.

"What remedy have you to suggest?" the King demanded of Cromwell, who shook his head in despair. Henry called in others of his advisers.

"Is there no remedy but that I must needs, against my will, put my neck in the yoke?" Henry asked. And when no one had any advice, he found his own remedy.

He married Anne of Cleves on January 6, 1540, but never lived with her, and finally obtained a divorce on July 9. Anne of Cleves placidly agreed, and settled down in England with a gift from Henry of two houses well staffed with servants and £500 a year.

Before the divorce was granted, Thomas Cromwell was suddenly arrested at a Council meeting. The King was angry over the fiasco of his marriage to Anne of Cleves, and blamed Cromwell. This gave Cromwell's bitter enemies, the Dukes of Norfolk and Suffolk, their chance.

Cromwell knew very well that they were responsible. He stood up at the Council table, quaking with rage, tore off his hat and hurled it to the floor. It was an empty gesture, for Norfolk and Suffolk were already stripping him of his decorations, and a boat was waiting to take him to the Tower.

Cromwell was stunned. He had thought the King had forgiven him for praising Anne of Cleves. In April, Henry had made him Earl of Essex and Lord Great Chamberlain of the Household. A treacherous man himself, he had forgotten that cruel Henry VIII could play the cat-and-mouse game too. The charges brought against him were partly half-truths and partly outright lies. Nevertheless, he was convicted of both treason and heresy, and beheaded on July 28, 1540.

No one took Cromwell's place. With Henry supervising, the Privy Council ran the government. But the King missed Cromwell's genius, and he also began to realize that he had been led astray by the minister's enemies, and showed his resentment against them.

The King's health was not good. About 1528 a painful ulcer had developed on his leg. No medicine helped it. Then, in 1536, he had a bad fall from his horse and was unconscious for two hours. And by the next year the ulcer had spread to the other leg. Also, because he gorged himself with food and drink, he had now grown into the hulking, square-built bull of a man so familiar from Holbein's famous painting of him. But underneath the powerful frame, Henry VIII was slowing down.

Now came the King's fifth wife. Catherine Howard, niece of the Duke of Norfolk, was nineteen, rather short and plump and, like Anne Boleyn, gay and vivacious; the King was thirty years older. Eighteen days after the divorce from Anne of Cleves, on the very day that Thomas Cromwell was executed, Henry and Catherine were married.

For a few months this fifth wife did wonders for the King. His ill health disappeared. He showered lavish gifts on his young bride, took her about proudly and held dances and banquets for her. He gave her all of Thomas Cromwell's extensive lands.

All this attention, homage and luxury could hardly fail to turn a young girl's head. The only strange thing is that Catherine Howard had learned no lesson from Anne Boleyn's death. It was bad enough that she became arrogant, but worse that she was careless about the attention shown her by handsome young gallants of the Court.

When Henry set out on a progress, his first visit to the north, Catherine's unfaithfulness to him was no secret to anyone at the Court but the King himself. And while he was away, an informer told the Council of a romance Catherine had had before her marriage.

Blithely ignorant of this, the King went north in great pomp and glory. All along his route he appeared before crowds of spectators, who saw a benevolent-appearing, jovial King. But just in case any revolts might be brewing, Henry brought along five thousand horsemen, one thousand soldiers and a train of artillery to show his might. Besides, he was going to meet King James V of Scotland in York to talk of peace, and this force would impress James too.

After reaching York on September 18, 1541, Henry waited nine days while the Scottish King did not appear. His advisers were afraid the English might kidnap him. Seething over this insult, Henry turned south and went back to Hampton Court. There, on November 1, Archbishop Cranmer arrived, bringing a document from the Council telling of Catherine Howard's infidelity.

"It is not true!" the King thundered. "It is a pack of lies!"

But at last, after an all-night meeting with the Council, he had to admit that evidence against his wife proved the charges beyond doubt. First Henry raged. "Fetch me a sword that I may kill her!" he raved. Finally he collapsed in tears.

In spite of the revelation, Henry was willing to let Catherine go free with a divorce, until still more unfaithfulness was proved against her. Henry's vengeance then was swift. On February 10, 1542, she was taken to the Tower. Charges drawn up against her were approved the next day, and on February 13 Catherine Howard was beheaded.

The King soon recovered from the shock of his loss. He itched to avenge the slap in the face he had received from the absent King James V at York, but he needed the Scots' neutrality so that he could join the Emperor Charles V in an attack on France, an ally of the Scots. There could be no invasion from the north to interfere.

But the Scots kept hedging. Finally they did invade the northwest of England with 20,000 men. In a battle on November 25, 1542, an English army routed them, slew many and took many prisoners.

With the Scots now so weak, Henry decided to go ahead with the French invasion. He himself crossed the English Channel, led an English army against Boulogne and captured it. He then returned to England, leaving the Dukes of Norfolk and Suffolk to continue the campaign. But treachery killed Henry VIII's great plan to subdue France. Charles V abandoned his English alliance and made peace with Francis I of France. The English had to return home.

Henry was in desperate trouble. He had both Francis I and Charles V to contend with now, and the Scots were again threatening to invade England, aided by a French army. To pay the tremendous cost of the war, the King had to levy "benevolences," or forced gifts of money, forced loans and heavy taxes. He added more and more base metal to English gold and silver coins. And he tried to borrow from money lenders in Antwerp.

Francis I prepared to invade England with a fleet of two hundred ships. More than 30,000 English soldiers were drawn up along the south coast. But while the French did make a few landings, they were driven back and at last, in August, 1545, the enemy sailed away.

England was saved, but the kingdom was near bankruptcy. Yet in 1546 Henry managed to obtain enough money to strike at France again. Then, after the army crossed to Calais, he suddenly changed his mind and signed a peace treaty with the French on June 7, 1546. The war had cost over £2,000,000, and all that England had gained was Boulogne to add to her little foothold in France at Calais.

The King had one consolation. In July, 1543, he had married his sixth and last wife, Catherine Parr. He could not have found a finer woman. Although she was no beauty and was widowed twice, she was intelligent and of the highest character. She gave Henry VIII tender devotion during the last years of his life, and her influence upon him was always for the good, something much needed by this man who had been so cruel and ruthless.

Catherine Parr united Henry VIII's family. It was no easy task to bring the three children and the King together. Elizabeth had been at odds with her father, and Mary was bitter because Henry had forced her to acknowledge his supremacy over the Church in England in spite of her devout Roman Catholic faith.

Henry's ulcer was now beginning to eat away his life. Although he was lovingly cared for by Catherine Parr, he could no longer walk. Servants carried him around in a chair and used a hoisting device to get him upstairs. In February, 1546, fever struck him down for three weeks, but he recovered enough to sit up and play cards with some of his Council. He even planned to make a long progress through all his kingdom, but while his mind was willing, his body was not.

As the Christmas season approached, Henry sent Catherine to Richmond Palace, where the holiday festivities would be held, but he remained at Whitehall, with only the Privy Council and some of his noble attendants at hand.

Henry VIII knew that his end was near. Nine-year-old Prince Edward would be King, of course, but who should rule England until the boy was old enough to do so? The King decided not to entrust it to one man, who might be tempted to seize the throne. By one of the changes Henry made in his will, a small group of his most trusted advisers was named to rule.

For a short time, in mid-January, 1547, the King rallied, but he relapsed again, and by the evening of January 27 his doctors knew that his death was a matter of hours. At last Sir Anthony Denny, Chief Gentleman of the Chamber, approached the King's bedside.

"To man's judgment, you are not like to live, your Majesty," he said softly. "I exhort you to prepare yourself for death."

"I have been much abused for my life past," the King murmured, "yet is the mercy of Christ able to pardon all my sins, even though they were greater than they be."

"Is there some learned man I may send you to confer withal and open your mind unto?" Denny asked.

"If there be anyone, it is Cranmer," replied the King, "but first I will take a little sleep, and then, as I feel myself, I will advise upon the matter."

When the King awoke, he knew his death was near. Cranmer

was sent for. The King's power of speech was gone now, but he put his hand in the archbishop's.

"Give me some token, your Majesty, that you put your trust in Christ," Cranmer said, and the King squeezed his hand. Then, at two in the morning of January 28, 1547, Henry VIII died at the age of fifty-five after reigning more than thirty-seven years. It was February 15 before a formal procession four miles long was formed and reached Windsor Castle, where he was laid to rest in St. George's Chapel.

Henry VIII was a tyrant who ruled relentlessly and seldom showed pity for those who opposed or betrayed him. A torrent of blood was shed in his reign, though far less than in the barbaric raids and bloody massacres of the time in Continental Europe. He bankrupted England with his extravagances and the wars he fought, and brought suffering upon his subjects through taxation and wringing money from them in other ways. At the end of his reign, he was no longer loved by the people.

Henry began the Reformation in England. True, in the light of what happened in the half century after his death, it was bound to come, anyway. If he had been satisfied to give his subjects freedom to worship as they wished, it would have been different. What Henry must be blamed for most was the looting, abolishment and destruction of the monasteries in his frenzied thirst for vengeance upon the Church of Rome.

Henry VIII was a strong king at a time when a strong one was needed. But for that, England might have fallen a victim to the greedy, treacherous rulers of other European nations, who would have struck at the slightest sign of weakness. There can be little doubt that he saved England from that. It is the best that can be said of him.

7

The Boy King and His Protector

BABY PRINCE EDWARD, HENRY VIII'S ONLY SON, remembered nothing of his mother, Jane Seymour, who had died so soon after his birth, and nothing of the pomp of his christening and baptism, either, in the chapel of Hampton Court Palace, by Archbishop of Canterbury Cranmer.

Nor would Edward have remembered the first journey he took with his proud father to the royal hunting lodge at Royston, for he was only seven months old; but the villagers there did. Always ready to endear himself to his subjects, Henry VIII spent much time in the nursery, and the people crowded around the windows, peering in to see their King fondly dandling his little son in his arms.

Edward was a healthy, beautiful little boy, with a fair complexion and gray eyes, and good-sized for his age. Everyone showered him with gifts. His half-sister, Princess Mary, old enough to be his aunt, was very fond of him and brought costly gifts when she came to Court. And by the time he was two, he and his other half-sister, Princess Elizabeth, then six, dearly loved each other.

For some years Edward was under the charge of Catherine Parr, who gave him the most loving care. But when the prince was six, the King brought in Richard Cox, head of the famous boys' school at Eton, as Edward's tutor, along with several others.

The prince's ABCs began with a hornbook that had colored letters. Hornbooks were used even then in England; a hundred years later, children in the American colonies used them too. A hornbook was a flat piece of wood, something like a small paddle, with a handle. On it was the alphabet in small and capital letters, and usually the Lord's Prayer. It got its name from its covering of a sheet of transparent horn to protect it from grimy young fingers. Edward also learned to write in a clear, simple hand, and to express himself clearly.

When Edward was four, he was stricken with a dangerous illness, but he overcame it. For a time he was separated from his sisters and rested at a royal palace in the country, with no lessons. After that, Edward spent most of his time at Hampton Court Palace, where his father and sisters were. Henry VIII dominated his children, as he did everyone. They loved and feared him at the same time, and his influence over them was reflected when, during later years, all of them in turn came to rule England. They had his ways and imitated his speech, and all could be imperious and demanding.

Edward followed much the same daily routine as his father— up at six, attending Mass in the chapel at seven, riding horseback or practicing shooting at targets in the orchard or, in wet weather, bowling in one of the galleries till ten o'clock.

Then came dinner, served with great pomp. After the Lord Steward had supervised the laying of the tablecloth, a procession of servants stood in line behind the table, holding pitchers of scented water, basins and towels, for forks were unknown and the guests had to wash their greasy fingers often.

To a great blast of trumpets, the royal family came in, each leading a guest by the hand. The first course was usually brawn—pressed, boiled, spiced and pickled boar or hog meat—with mustard, and soup. The main course was generally beef, mutton, vension, stuffed swans and goose. The servants then changed the plates, and the diners, who must already have been well filled, had meat pies of game birds. A clean tablecloth was then laid, and the diners washed their hands and had dessert—cheese, sweets, fresh fruits, biscuits and cakes. Supper was just as lavish. But Prince Edward had to be content with only a few dishes at each meal.

Music, dancing and outdoor sports and games were considered important to the young prince's education. Under his tutors he learned to translate and write Latin and Greek. He was required to read the Bible thoroughly, but he rebelled against learning the whole Book of Proverbs by heart. Painting, sculpture and other arts did not interest him, but he loved pageants with their brilliant costumes, and like his father he was fond of splendid clothes and sparkling, costly jewels. Edward worshiped Henry VIII.

Just how much the boy was told when Catherine Howard suddenly disappeared is not known, but he found an excellent substitute for a real mother in Catherine Parr. And he gained a lifelong friend when he was seven and friendly, witty John Cheke, one of the governors of Cambridge University, came to be his tutor.

Edward was eight when peace was signed between England and France in June, 1546. A painting of him at that time shows his delicate features, fine complexion, reddish-gold hair, gray eyes with long lashes and an air of dignity and grace.

Doubtless at this time he knew his father's health was not good, but there is no indication that he thought he would soon be King of England. During Henry VIII's last illness, Prince Edward was kept at the country palace of Ashridge. On January 29, 1547, his uncle, Edward Seymour, the Earl of Hertford, came there.

"We are going on a journey to the palace at Enfield, your Highness," the earl said. He did not tell Edward why.

In the Presence Chamber at Enfield, designed for solemn ceremonies, Edward found Princess Elizabeth waiting. Hertford said to Edward, "We have come to tell you of the death of your father, our beloved and excellent sovereign. You are King Edward VI of England, your Majesty. May God grant you a long and good life to the benefit of the realm of England!"

Neither Edward nor Elizabeth had known that their father was near death. Both burst into passionate weeping, clinging to each other.

The next morning Edward VI set out for London. At the Tower, he was met by its commander, the Constable, and Archbishop Cranmer and the lords of the Privy Council. In the Presence Chamber the nobles of the realm did the new King homage, with the crash and thunder of the Tower's saluting cannon seeming to make its thick walls quiver.

Early the next morning, before the Council, which had been meeting all night to discuss Henry VIII's will, Edward was asked: "Are you willing, your Majesty, that your uncle, the Earl of Hertford, be proclaimed Lord Protector of the Realm and Governor of your person until you become of age?" He agreed, not knowing that this was a clear violation of Henry VIII's will because it left the government in charge of a single man.

Then Hertford, followed by the other peers, knelt, kissed the young King's hand and said, "God save your Grace!"

"With the help of God and yourselves, I shall do my duty," Hertford promised the other lords, and each of them swore loyalty to both the King and the Protector.

Edward VI created his uncle, the new Protector, Duke of Somerset, and it is as Somerset rather than Hertford that this important man in Edward VI's life came to be known. The Protector's brother, Thomas Seymour, also Edward's uncle, was made Lord High Admiral of England.

On February 19, 1547, Edward VI was crowned in Westminster Abbey. The procession from the Tower was one of the most elaborate and gorgeous ever seen in London. Edward wore a gown of cloth of silver embroidered in gold, a doublet and half-boots, or buskins, of white velvet, and his white cap, perched at a jaunty angle, was so covered with gems that it seemed to be one blaze of fire in the sunlight. The streets had to be railed off to hold back the cheering thousands along the route. Edward was crowned first with St. Edward's Crown, used by William the Conqueror in 1066, then the Crown Imperial, so heavy that they merely held it over Edward's head, and finally a small copy of this second crown, made especially for him.

Actually, this beginning of Edward VI's reign was really the beginning of his uncle's, the new Duke of Somerset. Somerset had high intelligence and ability to rule, but his ambition was so consuming that as Protector he thought only of seizing more and more power. He allowed Edward VI little part in the government, keeping him busy with his studies under Cheke.

Somerset dominated both the young King and the Council. He grew arrogant. In letters and proclamations he began to use the "we" that was the sovereign's sole privilege, instead of "I."

Sometimes he issued royal proclamations without mentioning them to the King. He was insolent to foreign ambassadors. He wrote a letter to the King of France, calling him "brother." Francis I replied by instructing his ambassador at Westminster to remind Somerset that he was not the King of England, who might call the King of France "brother."

Before long Edward VI began to see through his uncle's schemes to put him in the background, though there was little he could do about it. Nevertheless, someone did think something could be done about it—Somerset's brother, Thomas Seymour, the new Lord High Admiral. This rascal was one of the handsomest men in England, a tall, dashing, bearded man who charmed everyone, especially women. He was as ambitious as his brother and insanely jealous of Somerset's power as Protector. He began to scheme to destroy Somerset and seize the protectorship for himself.

First, the admiral set out to win the young King's friendship and trust in order to turn him against Somerset. This crafty man placed a spy, Thomas Fowler, as an attendant in the King's private apartments, the Privy Chamber, to watch, listen and report all he learned to the admiral.

Thomas Seymour had been about to marry Catherine Parr when she took Henry VIII's fancy, so of course he had to give up that plan. But now Catherine was a widow. The admiral went to the boy King and said, "It is my great desire to wed your gracious stepmother, the Dowager Queen Catherine. Will your Majesty aid me?"

Like everyone else, Edward admired the admiral and he wrote his stepmother a letter in Seymour's behalf. Catherine not only accepted the admiral's proposal, but agreed to his suggestion that they be married secretly. Somerset did not suspect his brother of plotting against him, but when he finally learned of the marriage he was angry and gave the admiral a violent tongue-lashing.

Thus Seymour advanced closer to the King. Since his new wife kept apartments in the royal palace, he was able to see Edward more often. He won the boy King's trust, and Edward confided to him his chief complaint against Somerset—money.

Perhaps to teach Edward thrift, the Protector was stingy in doling out the boy's allowance of pocket money. The King, who loved fine clothes, jewels and other luxuries, was annoyed, especially when he learned that Somerset was obtaining rich grants of land for himself and had built a magnificent mansion, Somerset House, along the Thames, that was practically a palace.

Seymour sent the King a message through his spy, Fowler: "His Grace, the Lord High Admiral, hath asked me to say he will provide your Majesty with any sum of money that you need."

Edward did not accept immediately, but later he said to Fowler, "Have the goodness to express my thanks to my uncle, the admiral, and tell him that I should like some money now."

"What sum?" asked Fowler.

"As it pleaseth his Lordship," the King replied.

Thus Edward VI began to waver, not yet sure whether he should keep on trusting Somerset or put his reliance in the admiral. As for Seymour, he kept right on undermining the King's confidence in Somerset. At the time, the Protector was giving his full attention to arranging a marriage between Edward and the Queen of Scotland, four-year-old Mary Stuart. Nothing came of it, but the admiral made the most of his brother's inability to keep an eye on him.

One day he said to the King: "You must take it upon your-self to rule if you shall be able enough, as well as other kings."

Edward VI knew about royal prerogative—the special rights of a king to give commands that must be obeyed. The admiral, seeing that he had struck Edward in a tender spot, went on: "You are but even a beggarly king now. I will give Fowler money for you."

The admiral kept on sending cash to Edward. When the amount reached several hundred pounds, he thought he had the King where he wanted him. He demanded that Edward write a letter to the Council requesting that they make him Protector in his brother's place. The young King was in a trap, but he gave the admiral no answer.

Seymour then wrote the letter himself and gave it to Cheke, saying, "I would have you persuade his Majesty to sign this."

"I cannot do so, your Grace," the tutor replied firmly, and after the enraged admiral left, Cheke told Edward about it.

The young King showed he had courage. "The Lord Admiral shall have no letter signed or written by me," he said.

Seymour's great fault was that he could be foolishly rash, and he did not know when to keep his mouth shut. He ranted so much in public against his brother that Somerset became sus-picious and made it impossible for the admiral to see the King. With that, Seymour lost his temper completely. He organized a conspiracy to overthrow the government and seize the King and the protectorship for himself. Somerset had enemies, and they joined in the plot, but the reckless admiral could not wait for the conspirators to organize a force strong enough to seize the government. What he did was so harebrained that it seems like the idea of a madman.

The admiral was still at the palace, though the Dowager Queen, Catherine Parr, had died. One night he took a pistol and managed to creep into the Privy Chamber, where Edward was sleeping. He planned to kidnap the King and replace Somerset as Protector.

Edward's little dog was sleeping in a basket just outside the royal bedchamber. It awoke and began to bark. The admiral shot it dead, but that was the end of his wild scheme, for the whole palace was roused. Seymour was seized and arrested.

He was quickly condemned. Somerset refused to ask for mercy for his treacherous brother, and Edward VI approved his execution.

However, the admiral was popular with the people. Londoners were incensed when they heard that Seymour was to be beheaded. They called Somerset a "bloodsucker" and a "ravenous wolf." This gave Somerset's other enemies courage to continue their plot after the admiral's head was chopped off.

The conspirators were led by John Dudley, then Earl of Warwick and one of the greatest scoundrels alive. Early in October, 1549, Somerset learned of the plot. He immediately had handbills distributed throughout the kingdom calling on the people to defend the King and himself.

Somerset and Edward VI were at Hampton Court, guarded by five hundred of the Protector's men. Somerset dictated a letter, signed by the King, to two lords of the Council believed to be friendly, urging them to raise all the forces they could and come to the rescue. No answer came. Save for Archbishop Cranmer and three other lords, the Council had turned against Somerset.

The Protector then took Edward VI to Windsor Castle, still confident that he could regain his hold on the Council. Archbishop Cranmer did not agree. "It is my advice that you seek a meeting with the Council to reach an agreement," he said. "Otherwise, you risk civil war and the destruction of the kingdom."

The people of London now supported Somerset, for they hated the conspirators' leader, John Dudley. The Council sent heralds out to urge the Londoners to support them against the Protector. Dead silence greeted the announcements.

Somerset wrote the Council from Windsor saying that he did not intend to harm the King and wanted to reach an agreement. He also wrote John Dudley, reminding him of their old friendship, appealing to his loyalty and speaking of his long service to the Crown.

This last was like a lamb appealing to a hungry wolf. Dudley was determined to be Protector. The Council wrote Somerset to say that he would not be deprived of his honor or property if he would submit to arrest—a mere formality, they assured him.

No doubt Somerset knew this was an empty promise, yet he could do nothing but submit. On October 10 the lords of the Council arrived at Windsor Castle. Edward VI received them and presided over a meeting. They told him his uncle had deceived him, and showed their loyalty by kneeling and kissing his hand.

Three days later Somerset, his wife the duchess and one of his chief supporters were taken to the Tower of London. As they rode through the city streets, cheering mobs followed to the very gates of the prison-fortress.

Nevertheless, it was the beginning of the end for Somerset. A great change in the government lay before the boy King Edward VI.

8

Northumberland

THE FIENDISHLY CLEVER DUDLEY dared not destroy Somerset yet and risk a rebellion against himself by the people. Meanwhile, twelve charges had been brought against the fallen Protector. Edward VI wrote the Council, asking that his uncle's life be spared. The wicked, cunning Dudley told the other members, "My Lords, we must return good for evil. And as it is the King's will that the duke be pardoned . . . we ought to concede to his Grace's wishes." He meant nothing of the kind. He would simply bide his time.

Dudley used all his efforts to reassure the frightened King that no one would harm him, and that he himself wanted no power, just reform of the government. This was a barefaced lie, but Edward VI was soothed and his terror subsided.

Dudley assured the King that he would now have all the royal prerogatives Somerset had kept from him. There would be no Protector, and since the King favored the Protestant religion, Dudley swore that he too was a strong Protestant.

Dudley still feared Somerset's popularity with the people. On

February 1, 1550, the former Protector was released from the Tower on condition that he would not come within ten miles of the King, and would live as a private gentleman. Then, in April, his seized lands were restored, and he was readmitted to the Council and allowed to dine with the King. All this was the blackest kind of a scheme to hoodwink Edward into favoring Dudley.

Not only Edward, but Somerset himself was fooled. On June 3, 1550, Dudley offered more proof of his goodwill when his eldest son, Lord Lisle, was married to Somerset's daughter, Anne Seymour.

Dudley was now firmly established in power, though the young King did not realize it. He still had one deadly fear— Princess Mary, next in line for the throne under Henry VIII's will if Edward VI should die without an heir. Since Mary was a fanatical Catholic, and Dudley had cast aside his Catholic faith and declared himself a Protestant, his power if not his head would be lost if Mary became Queen. Somehow he had to be rid of her.

Mary had obtained Edward's permission to live quietly in the country, where her celebrations of the Catholic Mass could be winked at. Now Dudley began to stir up trouble over this. She complained to her half-brother, but Dudley was now in such full control that Edward did nothing about it. And when Emperor Charles V asked Mary to take refuge in Catholic Spain, Edward was incensed against both of them for interfering with his newly gained royal prerogative.

He summoned Mary to Windsor Castle. "Strange rumors have come to me about your Mass," he said sternly.

Defiantly, Mary declared that celebration of private Mass at her home was permitted, and began to cry. Edward, who still dearly loved his far older half-sister, also burst into tears. "I agree with her view," he sobbed.

Later, Mary appeared before the Council. "I hope his Grace will not be wroth with me till he is of an age to judge for himself," she said sarcastically. Edward was infuriated and angrily commanded Mary to obey him and stop her Masses.

Mary wrote back, "Rather than go against my conscience, I will lose my life."

Actually, the difficulty was that Mary's Mass was celebrated for all her household, making it public and thus punishable. Two of her chaplains were arrested and sent to the Tower.

Again Princess Mary was summoned to appear before the King and Council. As she rode into London, her attendants wore large rosaries over their doublets. London Catholics cheered her as she passed. This defiant act provoked both the Council and the King.

The meeting at Whitehall Palace was tense. After Mary had defended herself before the Council, she jabbed again at Edward VI's sore spot. "Riper age and experience will teach your Majesty much more yet," she said tartly.

Edward's reply too was sharp: "You may also have somewhat to learn. None are too old for that."

But when Mary repeated that she would die rather than give up her religion, the King replied, "I desire no such sacrifice."

The next day the Spanish ambassador handed an ultimatum to the Council from Charles V: if Princess Mary were not allowed to have her Mass, the Emperor would declare war on England.

War or no war, said Edward, Mary must obey him. The Council persuaded him to tell Charles V that the princess would be able to continue her Masses for a while, but later she would have to obey her brother.

All this trouble elated John Dudley. Meanwhile, a high honor was bestowed upon him, for Edward VI now trusted him fully. On October 7, 1550, he was created Duke of Northumberland, and this is how he was known from then on.

Somerset was one of Northumberland's attendants at the new duke's installation, but he was anything but easy in his mind about his future. He had heard certain things.

Northumberland had a secret agent, Sir Thomas Palmer, spying on Somerset. Palmer reported that for six months the former Protector had been organizing a conspiracy to regain his power. He was going to hold a banquet to which the Dukes of Northumberland and Suffolk and other lords were to be invited. All would be assassinated, said Palmer, the government seized and the King married to one of Somerset's daughters, and Somerset himself would again become Protector and bring the Catholic religion back to England. There were thirty-nine conspirators in the plot, he added.

This was a pack of outright lies, but it was enough for Northumberland. He rushed to the King and told him the whole story. Edward believed it. Then, at dinner following a Council meeting on October 16, the Lord Treasurer rose at the table. "My Lord Duke," he said to Somerset, "I charge you with high treason."

Guards seized Somerset and took him to the Tower. He was doomed, and he knew it. Northumberland, aware that the people's sympathy was with the former Protector, had him transferred from the Tower to Westminster at five in the winter-morning darkness of December 1, 1551. Yet word of it spread, and the Palace Yard was crowded with people.

"Justice for the duke!" they yelled. A thousand men-at-arms surrounded Westminster Hall. The crowd outside cursed Northumberland and the Council as Somerset faced his judges. The trial was a farce. The principal witness was Northumberland's spy, Palmer.

Somerset refused to cross-examine him. "You are a worthless villain!" he shouted. Then he simply denied the charges against him.

The lords of the Council debated Somerset's fate for six hours. The wily Northumberland asked that charges of high treason be dropped, and they were. He was afraid of what the people might do if Somerset were convicted on such ridiculous evidence.

Word that Somerset had been acquitted of high treason flashed outside to the waiting crowd. Its joyous shout is said to have been heard as far away as Charing Cross. But Somerset was not deceived. There remained charges of felonious treason. Of these, as he had been sure, he was convicted and sentenced to die.

Northumberland faced the prisoner, a grim smile of triumph curling his lips. "Oh, Duke of Somerset," he said, "you see yourself brought to the most danger and that nothing but death awaits you. . . . As for myself, I shall willingly forgive you everything, and will use every exertion in my power that your life may be spared."

This, too, was a vicious lie. It was said in the hope that people would not blame him for Somerset's death. As for the crowd outside, their rejoicing over what they had thought was Somerset's acquittal turned to despair.

Somerset waited several weeks in the Tower before the dread

summons came. Northumberland wanted to give the people's anger a chance to cool; also, there were the King's feelings to be considered. Edward VI was plunged into deep depression over the thought that his signature must doom his uncle. But Northumberland kept pointing out the danger of mercy.

"I myself," he told the King, "would wish the sentence commuted to imprisonment for life, your Majesty, but the risk is too great."

Still, the King hesitated for three days. Northumberland told him again that he must act, and at last Edward said gloomily, "Let the law take its course," and signed the death warrant.

The temper of the vast crowd assembled on Tower Hill on the morning of January 22, 1552, was ugly. A triple guard surrounded the scaffold. Somerset arrived, calm and stately. He mounted the scaffold and began to speak.

"I come hither to die," he said, "but a true and faithful man as any was unto the King's Majesty, and to his realm."

After speaking further at some length, Somerset knelt to pray. When he rose he shook hands with the sheriffs and the Constable of the Tower, and removed his collar and doublet. Then, according to the strange custom of the time, he handed the executioner his fee for the grisly work he was about to perform.

Somerset knelt again, put his head on the block and in a loud voice said three times: "Lord Jesus, receive my soul." Then the headsman's ax crashed down.

Northumberland was now easier in his mind. As for Edward VI, he was torn between awe and terror of the duke, and the trust this man was able to inspire in him in spite of his suspicion that Northumberland had made himself the real ruler of England.

If Henry VIII's will had been obeyed, and a group of Council members allowed to rule as regents, there is every indication that Edward VI would have made England a far better place had he lived and ruled for himself. Nevertheless, he did do some good. In February, 1552, Nicholas Ridley, Bishop of London, preached before the King at Westminster. A Protestant, he was famous for his liberal views and sympathy for the poor. In his sermon Ridley bitterly criticized the rich, greedy and hard-hearted nobles and high government officials for their lack of concern for the misery of London's poor. He told of starvation, crime and disease that raged in these wretched people's hovels down filthy alleys only a stone's throw from the mansions of the rich.

King Edward took notes as Ridley preached. Afterwards, he summoned the bishop for a conference.

"I would do good for these miserable people you speak of, my Lord Bishop," he said. "Fear not to speak out against the evils in my kingdom."

"The worst evils are in London, your Majesty," replied Ridley. "The dissolution of the monasteries, which ministered to the poor, has brought an appalling increase in overcrowding, dirt and especially disease, since it meant the closing of the hospitals administered by the Church. I pray you, your Majesty, consult with the Lord Mayor on a plan to aid these poor wretches."

"I agree with your Lordship," said the King. He commanded the Lord Mayor of London to come to the Court. That evening, with one of the Council, a plan was worked out following Bishop Ridley's suggestions. A committee of the city's aldermen was appointed to make the arrangements.

Edward VI had time to make a start, at least, with the plan.

Across the Thames, in Southwark, stood St. Thomas' Hospital, empty, beginning to crumble and almost uninhabitable. The King ordered it rebuilt, and money provided to reopen it. The same was done with the large establishment of the Grey Friars in the City itself. And Edward VI gave one of his own palaces, Bridewell, which became Christ's Hospital.

More might have been done but for the King's health. In April, 1552, he was stricken with what was probably the disease known today as measles. Although he threw it off, seemed healthy again and would never admit he was tired, he looked frail.

The people had not forgotten that Northumberland had sent the Protector to his death, and the duke knew it. When he decided that the King should go on a progress through Sussex, Hampshire, Wiltshire and Dorset, accompanied by the Court, he invented an excuse for remaining behind. He was afraid the people's hatred of him would ruin the purpose of the progress—to let the people see their young King and rejoice that he had come to visit them.

The journey was highly successful. In Wiltshire the procession turned back toward Windsor Castle by way of Salisbury. There Northumberland joined the party. He was shocked when he saw the King. Edward had been so magnificently entertained along the route that he was exhausted.

Northumberland was convinced that the King was doomed. Before him was the specter of the Catholic Princess Mary, next in line for the throne. So the duke embarked on a diabolical plot to keep both Mary and Elizabeth from the throne. The third in line under Henry VIII's will was Frances, Duchess of Suffolk, a strong-willed, ambitious woman who might take away Northumberland's power. But her daughter, Lady Jane Grey, was an innocent young thing who could easily be controlled. The duke devised a plan to seize Princesses Mary and Elizabeth and put Lady Jane Grey on the throne.

His first move was to get the King to summon a Parliament in February, 1553. It carried out Northumberland's wishes by declaring that although Edward was only fifteen, he had come of age with the full powers of a king.

In January, 1553, Edward VI had summoned Princess Mary to Westminster for the festivities in celebration of Candlemas Day, February 2. She was stunned to find the King in bed with congestion of the lungs, a high fever and breathing difficulty. There was no celebration, and Mary left the next day. She did not know she had seen her brother for the last time.

Edward's earlier attack of measles may have left him weakened and susceptible to other diseases. Like the dead uncle he had never seen, Prince Arthur, the boy King had tuberculosis, incurable then unless a person's constitution was powerful enough to throw off the disease.

After three weeks in bed, Edward seemed much better. But when at last he was able to attend a Council meeting, those who had not seen him since before his illness were filled with dread, for a weak, thin boy with death in his face sat before them. Yet the people, especially the Protestants, were relieved, for the rumor that he was dying had alarmed them lest the vengeful Catholic Mary should rule them. But the improvement was, and could be, only temporary.

Northumberland was going ahead with his evil, risky plan. Meanwhile, he artfully instilled into Edward's mind the idea that he was not likely to live long. In deep depression, fear and anxiety, the King clung to the only person he thought he could trust—Northumberland.

Edward VI's greatest worry was the succession to the throne. Because of his strongly Protestant religious faith, the Church of England had veered away considerably from the Catholic form of service used under Henry VIII. The thought of Catholic Mary's ruling England horrified him, for she would use all her power to bring the Church of Rome back to England.

He was also concerned over his plan to establish charitable institutions to help the poor, and to endow grammar schools so that poor children could be educated. The King made arrangements for these charitable acts before he left Westminster for the purer air of Greenwich Palace. The grammar schools still bear his name.

Princess Mary tried to visit her dying brother, but Northumberland kept her away. He did the same with Princess Elizabeth, and the letters she wrote Edward were never delivered.

Northumberland's objective was to get Edward VI to use his royal prerogative and rescind Henry VIII's will, which made Mary first and Elizabeth second in line for the throne if Edward left no children. He had no doubts about the King's attitude toward Mary. But he implanted in the dying Edward's mind the belief that since Henry VIII had lived with Anne Boleyn before his divorce from Catherine of Aragon, Elizabeth was illegitimate and could not be Queen.

Edward fought death with great courage and strength of will. By early May, 1553, he was able to read with his beloved tutor Cheke and receive the French ambassador, though he could hardly speak.

The English people, sure that the King was dying or was

perhaps already dead, were in a panic. Northumberland ordered Edward lifted out of bed and held up to a window so that the crowds outside would know he was still alive. The wasted figure they saw did not improve their hopes. And when Northumberland issued a proclamation saying the King was so much better that he could walk each day in the palace gardens, they did not believe his lie.

June came, and the King still fought for his life. In order to be ready to move quickly and put Lady Jane Grey on the throne, Northumberland somehow had to keep Edward alive a little longer. He dismissed the King's doctors and installed one of his own, along with a female quack doctor who claimed she could cure Edward.

The King was in the last stages of tuberculosis, and having hemorrhages in which he bled from the lungs. The quack dosed him with deadly arsenic, and while the hemorrhaging did stop, the King soon began to suffer agonies from the arsenic poisoning. Northumberland became alarmed and recalled the Court doctors. The fraudulent quack was never heard of again, and may have been murdered to keep her mouth shut.

One thing remained for Northumberland to accomplish: to get Edward VI to make a will leaving the succession to Lady Jane Grey. Having warned the King of the dangers to England in having either Mary or Elizabeth as Queen, he pointed out what a fine one Lady Jane would make. At last Edward gave the duke authority to draw up a will leaving the crown to her.

But the Lord Chief Justice, the Solicitor General and the Attorney General believed that the will was illegal, since Henry VIII had already designated first Mary and then Elizabeth as Edward's successors if he had no children. When they were called upon to sign the young King's will as witnesses, Sir Edward Montague, the Lord Chief Justice, said, "I cannot. Such an act would be high treason."

Quivering with rage, Northumberland shouted: "You are a traitor!" And since all three ministers feared for their lives if they refused, they signed, asking a pardon for doing so. Archbishop Cranmer, who also had to approve the will, did not wish to sign either, but he too finally yielded. Then Edward VI signed the will.

For fifteen days the stricken King lived. The arsenic made his arms and legs swell up, his hair and nails fell out and his fingers and toes became gangrenous. He was still conscious, though hardly able to breathe, and he prayed for death. Late in the afternoon of July 6, 1553, it came peacefully.

Northumberland kept the King's death a secret as long as he dared, while he and his conspirators prepared for their perilous move. The duke was in mortal terror that the secret of the arsenic might be discovered. Somehow he had to get rid of the body, lest the autopsy before it was embalmed reveal the poison.

No one knows what finally happened to Edward's body. Northumberland may have bribed those who performed the autopsy, though this was risky. Another story has it that the body of a young man who resembled Edward was substituted for that of the King, while the real body was buried secretly near the palace. At any rate, what are supposed to be the remains of Edward VI lie buried in Westminster Abbey.

At last, John Dudley, Duke of Northumberland, and the conspirators who had joined him were ready to place Lady Jane Grey on the throne of England.

9

The Nine-Day Queen

THE STORY OF LADY JANE GREY makes her the most pitiful of all of England's rulers. She is called a queen, though her reign lasted only nine days and she never had a real coronation. It is the story of an innocent, very religious young girl who was the victim of that unscrupulous scoundrel, Northumberland, and her own ambitious, greedy and vicious parents.

Lady Jane Grey was born on October 12, 1537, at her father's estate of Bradgate in Leicestershire. Her father, Henry Grey, at that time Marquess of Dorset, a handsome, well-educated man, had not done as well as he had hoped, but in 1533 he had grabbed at a chance to advance himself. It bothered him not at all to break his engagement to Lady Katherine Fitzalan in order to marry Lady Frances Brandon.

Frances, as has already been mentioned, was third in line for the throne after Edward VI under Henry VIII's will. She was far more crafty than her husband. As a girl she was considered a beauty, but as she grew older she became as coarse and brutal in appearance as the character that lay behind her looks. She dominated her husband, and he became her puppet.

The Dorsets, as by custom they were then known, had three daughters, the Ladies Katherine, Jane and Mary. Katherine was the beauty of the family. Jane was nice-looking, but small, with light hair and very fair skin that was marred by freckles, considered a disfigurement in those days. Lady Mary was dwarfish and ugly.

For all Lady Katherine's beauty, the Dorsets realized that Lady Jane was the real prize as far as an advantageous marriage was concerned. She was an extremely brilliant girl, attractive and far more gifted than her sisters in every way.

From the time Lady Jane was born, her artful mother began scheming for her marriage. Henry VIII's son and heir, Edward, was Lady Jane's age to the day. Why not arrange her marriage to him? Then Lady Jane would someday be his Queen. All through her girlhood, Lady Jane was not only trained for royal life, but treated as a princess, while her sisters were the Cinderellas of the household, allowed no luxuries and sometimes treated harshly by their mother.

As a child, Lady Jane must have loved Bradgate, for she had a true appreciation of beauty. From its stately mansion she could look out on a great park, shaded by ancient oaks. In the distance lay a pretty lake and the dense greenery of a forest. Around the mansion were carefully tended gardens, edged by a sparkling brook.

The house itself was magnificent, built of rose-colored brick with white facings. Its great hall was eighty feet long, with wings at each end. The Dorsets entertained there often at dinner. But when it pleased them to dine in view of guests of lower rank, they looked down on them in lordly state from a gallery overhead.

A meal at Bradgate was as ceremonious and sumptuous as those in royal palaces. But Lady Jane and her sisters did not grow fat and lazy on all this plenty and luxury. They rose in time for prayers at six. At all meals they were required to eat in silence. Breakfast was meat, bread and ale, and they were allowed only a few of the dishes served at other meals.

During the morning, the girls studied Greek and Latin, in the afternoon music, modern languages, classical books and the Bible. After supper they danced and did needlework till bedtime at nine. Now and then the monotony was broken when their parents took them out shooting or hawking. Occasionally there was a trip with their parents into the city of Leicester to pay social calls.

Meanwhile, Lady Frances was sparing no effort to marry Lady Jane off to Prince Edward. Her royal blood allowed her to be often at Henry VIII's Court, and she cultivated the friendship of Henry's last Queen, Catherine Parr. Thus, when she was nine or ten, Lady Jane became one of the Queen's attendants. Gracious, charming Catherine Parr became one of the few friends she ever had.

Lady Jane wore the richest of clothes—fashionable bell-shaped skirts of fine cloth interwoven with gold and silver, bodices and stomachers also of rich materials, with slashed sleeves so long that they nearly touched the ground and jeweled hoods from France that were the latest style.

Within a few weeks of Henry VIII's death, Catherine Parr's former suitor, Thomas Seymour, the Lord High Admiral, was courting her again. Such a thorough rogue was unworthy of a fine woman like Catherine Parr. And in his determination to replace his brother Somerset as Protector, the admiral reached the same conclusion as Lady Frances Dorset had about her daughter—why not Lady Jane Grey as Edward VI's bride? He approached the Dorsets with the idea, and they were delighted to join him in it. But when the admiral made no progress, Lord Dorset had a talk with him.

"Look you, my Lord Admiral," he said, "time is fleeting and naught comes of your plan. If you cannot wed the Lady Jane to his Majesty, we will remove her from the Dowager Queen Catherine's household and seek another marriage for her."

"Be not impatient, my good Dorset," replied Seymour. "My plans will be realized if you will give me a little time."

The greedy Lord Dorset, knowing how much the admiral wanted to achieve his aim, said, "It should be worth a goodly sum to you if the Lady Jane remains in the Dowager Queen Catherine's household so that you can betroth her to the King. How much will you pay?"

"Two thousand pounds when it is done," replied Seymour.

"Agreed—but I must have several hundred pounds in advance."

"Done," said Seymour, and he paid Dorset part of the money.

After Thomas Seymour and Catherine Parr were married, Lady Jane went with them to the admiral's country estate in Gloucestershire. But when Catherine died soon after giving birth to a daughter, Lord Dorset sent for Lady Jane to come home. Seymour, still sure he could marry her to the King, sought out the Dorsets.

"I will marry her to the King's Majesty," he swore. "If I might get the King at liberty"—he meant out of Somerset's grip—"I dare warrant you he shall marry her."

Dorset got £500 more out of Seymour, and the admiral got

Lady Jane back again. Then came his idiotic attempt to kidnap Edward VI in which he lived up to Princess Elizabeth's shrewd comment on him as "a man of much wit and little judgment." The moment the Dorsets heard of his arrest, they removed Lady Jane from his house and betrayed him to the Privy Council to save their own skins by giving evidence needed to try and condemn him.

For Lady Jane Grey this was the beginning of five years of brutal treatment, deception, betrayal and, finally, death. The Dorsets, thinking that all chances of her marrying Edward VI were gone, took vengeance on their innocent daughter, who had not had the slightest part in the conspiracy; even in her occasional meetings with King Edward, she had behaved like the humblest of his subjects.

Lady Jane became truly a Cinderella, with a devilish father and mother in place of a cruel stepmother. Whatever she did or said did not satisfy them. They taunted, threatened, pinched, slapped and rained blows on her. To an old friend Jane once burst out with her misery. "When I am in the presence of my father or mother . . . *I think myself in hell!*" she cried.

She only found peace in reading, writing or listening to music. She was always a strong Protestant, and her devotion to her religion became intense.

Then came a sudden change in the Dorsets' fortunes. The Duke of Suffolk died, followed by his two male heirs in an epidemic. His daughter Frances became the heir, and the Dorsets found themselves Duke and Duchess of Suffolk. The Suffolks, as they must now be called, could move in the highest circles and be closer to the King.

Meanwhile, the wicked Northumberland had accomplished

what Seymour had failed—Somerset's downfall and death, followed by his own complete domination over the boy King. Then came Northumberland's plot to keep his power once the young King died. He planned not only to place Lady Jane on the throne, but to marry her to his own son, Lord Guilford Dudley. During Edward's last weeks of life, although her parents had forced her to marry Lord Guilford, Lady Jane knew nothing of Northumberland's murderous activities, for she had fallen ill and gone to the royal palace at Chelsea, outside London, to recover.

Once the dead King was safely buried, Northumberland moved swiftly. He had already persuaded the Duchess of Suffolk to give up her claim to the throne in favor of her daughter. And on July 9, 1553, the Council obeyed the duke's command and sent Lady Mary Sidney to bring Lady Jane to London.

"I am ill and cannot go with you," Lady Jane said. She did not yet even know that Edward VI had died.

"It is necessary for you to go with me," Lady Sidney replied. "The Council has ordered it."

Mystified, Lady Jane went with Lady Sidney by barge to the palace of Syon House near London. They entered its great hall, but found it empty. At last Northumberland came in, followed by two nobles, who advanced toward Lady Jane, knelt and kissed her hand.

She was bewildered and dazed. Although she had known that Edward VI had not long to live, she had assumed that either Mary or Elizabeth would be the new Queen.

The duke then led the party into the Chamber of State. There the Duke and Duchess of Suffolk, Jane's husband, Lord Guilford Dudley, and his mother, the Duchess of Northumberland, were waiting. They knelt as Northumberland led Jane to a dais under a canopy.

Northumberland stepped forward and spoke. "As President of the Council, I do now declare the death of his most blessed and gracious Majesty, King Edward VI," he began. "But . . . let us take comfort by praising his prudence and for the very great care he hath taken of his kingdom at the close of his life, having prayed God to defend it from the popish faith, and to deliver it from the rule of his evil sisters."

Perhaps the truth had begun to dawn on Lady Jane, but her head was in such a whirl that it is unlikely she understood fully what all this meant.

The duke continued: "His Majesty hath well weighed an Act of Parliament wherein it was already resolved that whoever should acknowledge the Lady Mary or the Lady Elizabeth . . . as heirs of the Crown should be had as traitors. . . . His Majesty hath named your Grace as the heir to the Crown of England. . . . Therefore, you should cheerfully take upon you the name, title and estates of Queen of England, France and Ireland."

Lady Jane fell to the floor in a faint. When she recovered consciousness, she burst into tears. At last she faltered, "The crown is not my right, and pleaseth me not. The Lady Mary is the rightful heir."

Northumberland turned purple with rage. "Your Grace doth wrong to yourself and to your house!" he shouted.

Jane's father and mother then went after her. "You will do what is required of you in obedience to your parents!" the duchess stormed. Jane's husband, more gently, pleaded with her to accept.

At first she stood firm. But having been brought up never to disobey her father and mother, though in her heart she had only hatred and dread of them, she knelt and prayed to God for guidance. She finally became convinced that He approved her becoming Queen.

"For what hath been given me as lawfully mine," she prayed then, "may Thy Majesty grant me such spirit and grace that I may govern to Thy glory and service to the advantage of this realm."

Northumberland and her knavish parents had won. Soon gilded barges carried her, her family and the Council to the Tower of London. Crowds were massed on the riverbanks as the flotilla reached the Tower. Its cannon roared a salute to the new Queen as she stepped ashore, stately in a gown of white and green, the Tudor colors, and embroidered in gold and silver, a white cap on her head heavy with diamonds, emeralds, rubies and pearls.

Since she was so small, they strapped wooden clogs three inches high to her feet so that the people might see her better. But this was a wasted effort, for there were no shouts and cheers of rejoicing; from the watching thousands came no sound at all. It was not that they disliked this girl, of whom they knew little. But they knew that Northumberland—this dictator and rogue whom they hated so bitterly—had put her on the throne. Yet at the Tower, even the modest, shrinking Lady Jane was impressed with the welcome given her.

On the threshold of the White Tower stood the Marquess of Winchester, Lord Treasurer of England, and Sir John Bridges, Lieutenant in command of the Tower, surrounded by officials and the Yeomen of the Guard in their medieval scarlet dress.

Henry VII.

Elizabeth of York, wife of Henry VII.

Henry VIII.

Queen Anne Boleyn

Queen Jane Seymour

The coronation procession of Edward VI.

Lady Jane Grey entering the Tower.

Preaching from the English Bible in a village during Tudor times.

The Duke of Buckingham and Cardinal Wolsey.

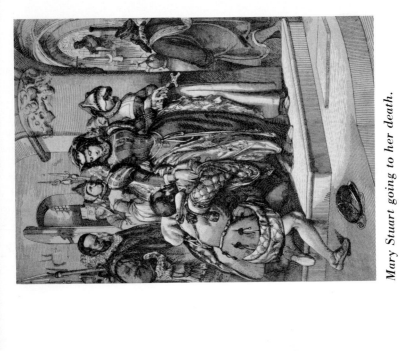

Queen Elizabeth I signing the death warrant of her cousin, Mary, Queen of Scots.

Mary Stuart going to her death.

Winchester stepped forward to hand the new Queen the keys to the fortress, but Northumberland intercepted him, seized the keys and gave them to Lady Jane. The meaning was plain: "I, John Dudley, Duke of Northumberland, grant this symbol of authority to the Queen."

The cannon were deafening. Flame and smoke belched continually from their muzzles. The smoke hid the White Tower's cupolaed turrets and drifted down on the Tower Green. In the Presence Chamber of the White Tower under the state canopy, the new Queen was presented with many jewels by Winchester. But when he tried to put the Crown Imperial on her head, Lady Jane refused.

"It would never have been demanded by me, or anyone in my name," she said.

At last she agreed to try it on, "just to see how it fits."

"Another shall be made to crown your husband," Winchester told her. And with that, all but Lord Guilford Dudley left the chamber. Lady Jane's jaw was set with the resolution she could show when she had to. "I shall not make you King," she told her husband. "Only by an act of Parliament can it be done."

"I will be made King by you and by Parliament," Guilford insisted. But Jane could not be moved. Northumberland's weak son then burst into tears and rushed out of the chamber.

Lady Jane called in two of the Council. "If the crown really belongs to me, I would be content to make my husband a duke," she said, "but I will never consent to making him King."

Just then Guilford and his mother stormed into the room. The duchess poured a torrent of abuse on the fifteen-year-old Queen, while Guilford whined and reproached her.

113

"I will make you a duke, but no more without the consent of Parliament," Lady Jane told him firmly.

"I will not be a duke; I will be King!" Guilford wailed.

"You shall live no longer with your wife!" the duchess ordered her son. And both left, choking with fury.

Two days passed. Lady Jane remained in her lodgings, tortured by doubts and fears. Was the crown really hers? She had no trust in Northumberland. And what of Princesses Mary and Elizabeth? How could she have a better claim to the throne than they?

Meanwhile, seeing that raging would not help them, the Duke and Duchess of Northumberland and Guilford Dudley came to dine with Lady Jane, accompanied by her mother. In the midst of supper, a messenger arrived with a letter from Princess Mary. She was on her way to London and demanded that Lady Jane surrender the throne to her.

The Duchesses of Northumberland and Suffolk gave way to sobs and torrents of tears. Lady Jane Grey said not a word.

During the next two days the young Queen knew little except that Northumberland, at the head of an army, had gone to intercept and capture Princess Mary. But she felt sure that if the duke failed, she would be executed for high treason.

Although Lady Jane did not know it, some of the Council were getting ready to desert her, support Mary and save their skins. The list grew steadily. The rats were deserting what they now considered a sinking ship.

On their march, Northumberland's men began to desert in droves, terrified lest they swing from the gallows if the attempt to capture Mary failed. On the night of July 16, 1553, the Earls of Winchester and Pembroke left the White Tower, never to return. On the 18th the Council left to meet at Baynard's Castle. They too did not return.

Left in the Tower were Lady Jane, her husband, her father and mother and the Duchess of Northumberland. All had been duped by the members of the Council, who at their meeting decided to keep their heads if possible by declaring Mary the rightful Queen of England, and Northumberland a traitor.

They also sent word to the Duke of Suffolk that his daughter's reign was over. He burst in on Lady Jane at supper and ripped down the canopy under which she sat.

"You are no longer Queen!" he cried. "We must put off your royal robes and be content with a private life."

"I much more willingly put them off than I put them on," she replied. "Out of obedience to you and my mother I have grievously sinned. Now I willingly relinquish the crown." And she added, "May I go home?"

Her father did not answer. Lady Jane was a millstone around both his own and his wife's necks. Let her look out her herself. By leaving her a prisoner in the Tower, he and his duchess might prove they were, after all, loyal to Mary. It might even save their lives. He, Lady Jane's mother and the Duchess of Northumberland then deserted her with no thought but for their own safety.

With four attendants, Lady Jane was then removed from the White Tower to a lodge on the Green under the supervision of the official jailer. Her husband was locked up in the Beauchamp Tower.

Winchester, who had welcomed Lady Jane so humbly, called

on her. "You are required to give up the Imperial Crown formally," he told her icily, "together with everything you have received from the royal wardrobe."

For some days Lady Jane Grey had unwillingly been Queen of England. Now she was nothing, deserted by her own parents and all who had been a part of the conspiracy to put her on the throne. Cowards all, they had left her to her fate. They lived now in terror, thinking only of somehow escaping the headsman's ax.

And what would this fifteen-year-old girl's fate be? That she would be tried, convicted and sentenced to death for high treason seemed certain. Only the new Queen could save her. Could she expect mercy from this onetime good friend, a fanatical Catholic who hated Protestants just as much as Lady Jane Grey hated Catholicism?

10

Bloody Mary: The First Years

THEY CALLED HER BLOODY MARY, and indeed torrents of blood spouted from the headless necks of many who were executed during her reign. But it was even more infamous for the stench of burning human flesh—hundreds of "heretics" died horribly at the stake rather than accept Mary Tudor's restoration of the Church of Rome to England.

Yet Mary I of England was neither a bloodthirsty nor a vengeful woman. Mary was bitter when she came to the throne after years of undeserved persecution, and rabid in her devotion to the Catholic religion, but she was not completely to blame for the terror that enveloped all England, and she was merciful and tender to many.

Her childhood was one of the two happy times of her life. Much as he wanted a son, Henry VIII loved his little daughter, born at Greenwich Palace on February 18, 1516, before his marriage to Catherine of Aragon broke up. Mary imitated many of his ways and had much of his looks, but always she was closest to and influenced most by her Spanish mother.

Being heir-presumptive to the throne when she was born, Mary was made Princess of Wales. At ten she had her own household at Ludlow, in the west near Wales. Her education, training and daily routine were much like those of her half-sister, Elizabeth, and half-brother, Edward, born so much later. At Ludlow she was happy.

The young girl's troubles began when her father cast off Catherine of Aragon for Anne Boleyn, who was to become Mary's bitter enemy. For a time she was with Catherine, who was exiled to Windsor Castle, but heartbreak followed when she was separated from the mother she loved so dearly.

For a time she and Catherine were able to write to each other. Mary was then at Greenwich Palace with the King and Anne Boleyn. Her father had turned against her now, and she bore many insults from both him and Anne. She was forbidden to correspond with her mother, though the two managed to do so secretly.

In September, 1533, just after Princess Elizabeth was born, Mary was told that she was no longer Princess of Wales because her father's marriage to Catherine of Aragon was not legal. In December the Duke of Norfolk came with a message from the King: "It is his Majesty's pleasure that you be removed to Hatfield to become an attendant to the Lady Elizabeth, the Princess of Wales."

"That is a title which belongs to me by right," the seventeen-year-old Mary retorted. Nevertheless, she was taken to Hatfield, north of London in Hertfordshire, but she refused to pay her respects to Elizabeth.

The King was enraged. Mary was given the worst room in the country palace, not allowed to go to Mass and persecuted by

Mistress Sheldon, Anne Boleyn's aunt, who was in charge of the household. She had only one servant now.

In 1534 Parliament passed the Act of Succession. It declared Mary illegitimate and gave the succession to the crown to the children of Henry VIII and Anne Boleyn. Mary steadfastly refused to acknowledge it. When Princess Elizabeth and her household went to another country palace, they had to put Mary in a litter by force to make the journey. She was persecuted even more when she refused to take an oath to obey the Act of Succession, although Mistress Sheldon told her the King had said he would have her beheaded if she refused.

When Mary fell seriously ill, Henry VIII did agree to have her placed in a house near her mother. After her recovery she was happier, but both she and her mother were shocked when Henry broke with the Pope and had himself declared Supreme Head of the Church in England. Then, on January 7, 1536, Mary suffered a terrible blow when Catherine of Aragon died. Her mother had been almost the only friend she had in England.

About this time, the King's affection for Anne Boleyn waned, and his fancy turned to Jane Seymour. As Henry VIII's third Queen, Jane Seymour tried to make peace between him and Mary, but Henry was determined to force his older daughter to obey him. The years of persecution had shattered Mary's nerves and health. She could not sleep and suffered the agonies of neuralgia. But when three envoys from the King tried to frighten her by threats into taking the oath, she refused. Henry's rage was terrible.

Mary still had one friend she felt she could trust, Eustace Chapuys, Charles V's ambassador to England. He had supported her strongly in her battle with her father, but now he advised her to submit. Her conscience could be easy, he said, since she was taking an oath under threat of force.

Mary gave in and acknowledged her father as Supreme Head of the Church in England, and agreed that her mother's marriage had been illegal. But once she had done it, she suffered torments for being false to her mother and her mother's church, which was also her own.

The King was pleased and ready to forgive. He and Jane Seymour came to see her and stayed overnight. Henry was gracious, gave Mary about a thousand pounds "for pocket money" and told her not to worry about expenses. The Queen was very kind and gave her a diamond ring. Mary's household was re-established at Hunsdon, and she spent Christmas with her father and stepmother at Greenwich Palace.

Now it was the executed Anne Boleyn's daughter, Elizabeth, who was neglected, while Mary was received kindly at Court. But she was not happy, for she believed her mother had been poisoned, and the signing of the oath still haunted her. She lost a good friend when Jane Seymour died after giving birth to Prince Edward.

Mary did enjoy some peace during the last years of her father's life. Henry was happy, with a son to succeed him, and she was now assured of succession to the throne if Edward should die without children. And for the first time since Elizabeth's early childhood, they were affectionate friends again.

When Henry VIII died, the Church was still Catholic in form despite its break with the Pope. But the greater reform under the devout Protestant Edward VI, and Mary's bitter opposition, brought her new troubles already described. She left the Court and lived in one of the manor houses Henry VIII had bequeathed to her. She got Charles V to make his demand upon the Protector for permission to use the Catholic service. At last Somerset said, "Well, she shall do as she thinks best until the King comes of age."

But John Dudley, later to become the infamous Northumberland, prodded the Council into ordering Mary to stop Masses for the whole household, since public ones were forbidden under heavy penalties.

"My house is that of my flock," Mary retorted, "and I will stand by my servants in doing their duty." Then she ordered her chaplains to say three instead of two Masses daily. There followed the struggle with Edward VI in which she did not yield.

Just before Edward died, Northumberland summoned Mary and Elizabeth to London to get his hands on them and then put Lady Jane Grey on the throne. Mary reached Hoddeston in Hertfordshire July 6, 1553. That day, Edward VI died. In spite of Northumberland's efforts to keep it secret, Mary learned of it that same night.

She knew she was in great peril and decided to head for the coast, where she might escape to the Netherlands if necessary. She also wrote Northumberland, claiming the throne, though she saw no possibility of overcoming him if he came after her, as he did.

But when Mary reached Framlingham Castle in Suffolk, as if by a miracle men began flocking to her support. Soon afterwards, Northumberland's force began to melt away, the Council in London deserted him and he himself was arrested.

Mary was Queen. She reached London in the evening of August 3, 1553, and went to the Tower, where her predecessor, Lady Jane Grey, was already a prisoner.

Mary Tudor was thirty-seven, a small, thin, frail, tight-lipped woman. Her face was lined by suffering, but her beautiful reddish hair and fair complexion gave her something of a youthful appearance. Her eyes were gray. She spoke in a loud, deep voice, almost like a man's. Her regal air proclaimed her a true Tudor; so did her short temper. But by nature she was a simple, sincere person. She had always liked to have supper with common people in country cottages and hear their problems.

To turn England back to Catholicism was Mary's chief concern. She chose her ministers from among those who would go along with her plans. Her Chancellor was Stephen Gardiner, whom she released from the Tower, where Edward VI had imprisoned him for supporting the old religion too strongly. He was honest, staunch in his opinions, had much common sense and understood the English people. Too often, Mary's quick temper kept her from listening to his good advice.

Meanwhile, the matter of Northumberland, Lady Jane Grey and the others in the wicked duke's plot had to be settled. Northumberland, his three sons and his brother, with several other conspirators, were quickly tried and condemned, though only the duke and two others not related to him were executed then.

Northumberland came before his judges in Westminster Hall, jammed to capacity. He was preceded, as was customary in treason cases, by the headsman bearing his ax, its blade turned away from the prisoner. The duke, believing his life would be spared, pleaded guilty to all the charges against him. As he was sentenced to die, the blade of the ax slowly turned toward him, again according to custom.

Northumberland then used all his influence and every trick in his bag to escape death. But when he called Gardiner to the

Tower to plead for his life, the Chancellor told him: ". . . To speak plainly, I think you must die." Gardiner did beg Mary to show him mercy, but on the advice of her Spanish friend and adviser, the new imperial ambassador, she signed the death warrant.

On the morning of August 23, 1553, Northumberland's head was lopped off on the scaffold on Tower Hill before an immense crowd. If ever a man in English history deserved his punishment, it was John Dudley, Duke of Northumberland.

Others were executed soon after him, but Lady Jane Grey remained in the Tower, confined in a house where the Gentleman-Gaoler lived. Close by, in the Beauchamp Tower, her husband, Lord Guilford, was still imprisoned.

The Queen, knowing she would have to have her subjects' goodwill, intended to let them worship as they pleased, convinced that God would show the Protestants the error of their ways and they would return to the Catholic faith. On August 12 she published a declaration saying that "she meaneth graciously not to compel or constrain other men's consciences."

But trouble was already brewing. When an old priest celebrated Mass at St. Bartholomew's, he was set upon and nearly killed. When another preached in St. Paul's churchyard, a mob shouting "Kill him! Kill him!" was driven off with much difficulty. And a shower of leaflets descended upon London, urging an end of loyalty to the Queen and Gardiner's destruction.

Strangely, Mary's coronation went off without hostile demonstrations. The Queen left the Tower on September 28 in the usual procession. Riding in a chariot drawn by six horses, she was radiant in a blue velvet gown trimmed with ermine, her red-gold hair covered with a net blazing with jewels and circled by a golden hoop. Crowds turned out to see her pass. Then came the solemn ceremony in Westminster Abbey, with a lavish dinner afterwards.

After Mary's declaration about freedom of worship, her first Parliament was surprised when it met and heard Chancellor Gardiner announce that the Queen was determined on submission to the Pope. A little later, when Mary asked Parliament to repeal her father's divorce from Catherine of Aragon, the members rebelled. They would agree only if the Queen dropped her plan to re-establish the Pope's supremacy. Mary decided to wait for her next Parliament before bringing up the subject again.

Parliament did pass some of Mary's requests concerning religion, however, the most important being that after December 20, 1553, the Catholic form of service used in the last years of Henry VIII's reign should be re-established in all churches. It caused great dissatisfaction among the Protestants. A dead dog with its head shaved and a rope about its neck was flung into the Queen's Presence Chamber, and more pamphlets against Mary, issued by the Protestants, littered the streets of London.

Mary was under much pressure to marry. Her chief suitors were Edward Courtenay, Earl of Devon, and Charles V's son Philip. Courtenay's father had been executed for treason during Edward VI's reign, and the son had spent fifteen years in the Tower until Mary released him at the age of twenty-seven.

He was hardly a fit husband for her, being frivolous and vain and lacking a strong character. Yet the Council tried to persuade her that Courtenay, as an Englishman, would be her best choice. Mary had other ideas. She did not decide for some time, but once she had made up her mind to marry Prince Philip, nothing could change it.

On November 16, 1553, an alarmed delegation from Parliament and the Council called on Mary to warn her that the people would resent and fear a Spanish husband, that Spain's great enemy, France, would be angered and that the religious question in England could never be settled if she married a prince of the most strongly Catholic country of Europe.

Mary flew into a terrible rage. "If you force me to marry one not to my liking it will mean my death," she stormed, "for I will not live three months, and I will have no children, and you will defeat your own ends." Then she gave Gardiner a tongue-lashing for leading the opposition to her chosen husband. He burst into tears and dropped the idea of marrying her to Courtenay.

All over the country, people seethed with anger over her choice, especially the Protestants. But the Queen plunged on heedlessly, and on January 12, 1554, the marriage treaty with Philip was signed.

It nearly cost Mary her crown. A conspiracy arose in which uprisings were planned in the west, the Midlands of Leicestershire, Wales and Kent. Lady Jane Grey's father, the Duke of Suffolk, was going to repay the Queen's mercy in sparing his life by leading the Leicestershire rebels. Courtenay too was in the plot. And the one who was to be the most important of all, Sir Thomas Wyatt, was to lead the Kentish rebels.

Courtenay made the mistake of ordering a coat of mail in London, arousing the Council's suspicions. He was seized and confessed what he knew of the plot. One leader was promptly arrested; another managed to flee to France. The treacherous Suffolk tried to get out of the country but was caught in hiding and later executed.

Only Sir Thomas Wyatt was left. As a youth he had led a

wild life and had been imprisoned in the Tower. But he had returned from service with the English army in France a seasoned soldier, officer and leader, tenacious and doughty.

On a market day in Maidstone, Kent, Wyatt read a proclamation warning the people gathered there that if the Queen married Philip, the Spaniard would bring in his troops to subdue and rule England. Men flocked to Wyatt's support. He then moved to the city of Rochester, where his force increased to 1,500 men, with more promised.

Then, at Gravesend, Wyatt made a master stroke. The captain of a squadron of English warships anchored there joined the rebel leader with his sailors, bringing along the ships' big guns. Wyatt then decided to march straight for London, sure that his friends there would throw open its gates. He now had four thousand men. They camped a little down the Thames and across from London.

The city was panic-stricken. The Council urged the Queen to leave, but she insisted on staying. Meanwhile, royal messengers were sent down the river for a parley. Wyatt was sure he had London in his pocket, and he replied with harsh terms: the Tower must be put under his control with the Queen in it; several Councillors must be removed and replaced by others of his own choice.

His demands were refused, and he marched his men to Southwark, just across London Bridge from the city. Meanwhile, Queen Mary herself made an appeal to the Londoners to stand with her and defend the city. She made them this promise about her marriage to Philip: "If this marriage should not seem advisable to all the nobility and commons in the high court of Parliament . . . then I will abstain from marriage while I live." The people believed her, and twenty thousand men stood ready to defend London and their Queen.

The drawbridge section of London Bridge was cut loose and the city's gates locked. Detachments were sent out from the city to destroy all the Thames bridges for fifteen miles above London. But at Kingston, Wyatt's army found a bridge whose pilings the Queen's men had neglected to destroy. They managed to repair it well enough for the army and the big guns to cross.

Wyatt's best chance of success was to reach London before dawn and take it by surprise, but because of his exhausted army's slow pace and the breaking down of one of the gun carriages, it was eleven in the morning when they approached the city from the west. A force of the Queen's cavalry and infantry barred the way to Newgate, where Wyatt had word that friends would open the gate. There was a fight with the royal defenders, but Wyatt managed to push through Fleet Street to Ludgate. Although it was locked, he knocked, hoping in vain that his friends might be there.

He turned and led his men back to Charing Cross, where the fighting began again. A herald called him to: "Yield, rather than be the death of all these, your soldiers. Perchance you will find the Queen merciful." Wyatt saw that he had no chance, and surrendered. He was taken to the Tower, followed by batches of his men. The rebellion, which might have been successful if he could have had the support of the other conspirators, was over.

Things now looked bleak for Lady Jane Grey, since both her father and her uncle were involved in the plot. Mary did not want to execute her, but the Spanish ambassador and some of the Council convinced her there could be no peace in England while Lady Jane lived. The Queen then signed the death warrants of both Lady Jane and her husband, Guilford.

Guilford went first to the scaffold on Tower Hill on February 12, 1554. From her window, Lady Jane watched him go. Later, as his body, with the severed head wrapped in a cloth, came back to the Tower in a cart, she saw this grisly spectacle too.

Nevertheless, Lady Jane went calmly to her death—on the Tower Green, since she could be executed privately because of her royal blood. There she granted the executioner's plea for forgiveness, saying only, "I pray you, dispatch me quickly." Then she knelt, saying, "Lord, into Thy hands I commend my spirit," and the ax fell. The executioner held up the head, crying, "So perish all the Queen's enemies! Behold the head of a traitor!"

She was no traitor, this innocent victim of her father, mother and the vile Northumberland. This was one of the most terrible injustices in England's history.

Sir Thomas Wyatt was beheaded on Tower Hill on April 11, 1554. Many other conspirators were hanged on gibbets set up all over London and in Kent as a grim warning. Yet some four hundred lesser prisoners, going down on their knees before the Queen, were pardoned.

Meanwhile, at the opening of the Queen's second Parliament on April 2, Chancellor Gardiner announced the signing of the marriage contract to Philip. He promised that the Spanish prince would take no part in the government. He asked that Mary be allowed to dispose of the succession to the crown in her will, as her father had done; but to this Parliament would not agree.

Meanwhile, Prince Philip dallied. He did not want to marry this woman, who was so much older than himself. He was doing it only because he felt it was his duty to Spain, and with a simple objective: to obtain control of England for his country. On the other hand, Mary was already pretty well in love with him after seeing his portrait.

At last the prince sailed from Spain, arriving off Southampton on July 19, 1554. Meanwhile, Mary had rushed to nearby Winchester to await her husband-to-be. There, on the evening of July 23, Philip went by torchlight to a gallery where Mary waited, resplendent in a gown of black velvet, and petticoat of frosted silver, with many jewels in her girdle and collar flashing in the light of candles.

Mary saw a small man of fair complexion, broad brow, large blue eyes, yellow hair and beard, with a royal bearing. In that instant the Queen fell madly in love with Philip of Spain. That love did not fade to the day of her death.

She led him to a canopy of state, where they sat down and talked, she in French and he in Spanish, since he knew no English. Then, two days later, they were married in Winchester Cathedral. A sumptuous banquet followed at which the bride and groom ate from plates of solid gold.

Against the will of her subjects and many advisers, Mary I of England had had her way. Now, for the second and last time in her life, she was gloriously happy. The stage was set for one of the most frightful periods in all English history.

11

The Terror

ALMOST FROM THE TIME Prince Philip and Queen Mary reached London after a leisurely journey down the Thames valley, there was trouble. When they reached the city the crowds were not unfriendly, but both Philip's Spanish retinue and the Londoners were soon grumbling.

Philip's Spaniards were put in the background, and a completely English household was established for him. The Londoners resented the Spaniards' presence and sometimes attacked them in the streets. They retaliated by complaining that they were being overcharged by shopkeepers who took advantage of the visitors' lack of familiarity with English money. And a horde of Spanish artisans had followed the Prince to England, causing a great hue and cry from London artisans, who feared the loss of business and jobs.

Philip was determined to be crowned as Mary's King. It would give him more power to prod England into war with Spain's enemy, France. Baron William Paget, Gardiner's enemy and a schemer for power, advised Philip to work to obtain a Council that would go along with his ideas, pointing out that the Queen was inexperienced in political affairs. Being in love with Philip and trusting him, she would take his advice and let him make the decisions, although they would seem to come from her.

Mary was perfectly willing to let her adored husband manage affairs of state while she, as Queen, merely approved what was done. Philip, of course, favored the plan to restore the Church of Rome as England's official religion. Gardiner favored it too, and felt that Reginald, Cardinal Pole, was the man to accomplish it.

Pole had been in exile for twenty years after breaking with Henry VIII over the split with Rome. Now, at fifty-three, he wanted to return to England. This member of a noble English family was a brilliant man, aristocratic, handsome, with a kindly manner.

The Pope made Cardinal Pole a papal legate to England. He arrived in London in November, 1554, and was welcomed by a delegation of bishops and lords—and Philip, who took him for an audience with Mary.

Parliament approved Pole's return, and within a few days England was Roman Catholic again after twenty years. All the changes Henry VIII had made were repealed, including the Act of Supremacy. Parliament refused to crown Philip of Spain as King of England, but it did provide that if Mary had a child and then died, Philip should govern as regent until the child became of age.

There was still Princess Elizabeth to be dealt with. If Mary died without children, Elizabeth would be next in line for the throne. Philip's calculating and—so he thought—simple solution for that was simply to marry Elizabeth if Mary died.

Now, he thought, was the time to get Elizabeth to accept the Catholic faith. At the end of April, 1555, she was brought to Hampton Court Palace. Philip welcomed her, but she did not see the Queen, and her apartments were guarded. Mary suspected that Elizabeth had had some part in the plot to overthrow her which had resulted in Wyatt's rebellion.

Next the Chancellor and some of the Council urged Elizabeth to submit herself to Mary's mercy, which would have amounted to a confession of guilt in the plot. Elizabeth dodged giving them an answer. Then, one night in May, she was summoned to the royal apartments, where Mary lay in bed. Elizabeth fell to her knees, declaring that she was innocent of any wrongful intent against the Queen.

Mary implored her to confess her part in the plot, but Elizabeth would say only, "I have borne the burden and must bear it. I humbly beseech your Majesty to think me ever to be your true subject . . . forever as long as life lasteth." With that Queen Mary had to be content, for Elizabeth soon left for one of the country palaces.

Someone had to enforce the new laws making the Catholic religion supreme and imposing death on all who refused it. This was left to the bishops who had accepted it. But the strong faction of Protestants in England was determined to fight it—to the death, if necessary.

The terrible three years of persecuting, hunting down and executing "heretics" who refused to become Catholics, which won the Queen the name of "Bloody Mary," had begun. The first to be executed was John Rogers, canon of St. Paul's, in February, 1555. The next month John Hooper, Bishop of Gloucester, and two country preachers were burned alive at the stake. In March it was Robert Farrar, Bishop of St. David's in Wales.

When Bishop Hooper was brought to the stake in the shadow of his cathedral in Gloucester, a crowd estimated at seven thousand was gathered there, for it was market day. Many were weeping. As the bishop knelt to pray, a box containing a pardon from Queen Mary if he would turn Catholic was set before him.

"If you love my soul, away with it, away with it!" the brave man cried.

They used dry reeds to light the fire, but the bundles of sticks, called fagots, piled around the stake were of green wood and would not burn. They brought drier ones, but a violent wind was blowing that day, and this second fire only burned off the bishop's hair and scorched his skin a little.

Hooper, like some others who went to the stake, had concealed bladders filled with gunpowder under his arms and between his legs in the hope that they would spare him slower death in the fire by exploding. But they burst open in the third fire that was built, and the fierce wind blew the burning powder away. Hooper's courage never failed him. He beat on his breast until his arm fell off, and then beat on it with the other until he died, after three-quarters of an hour of agony.

That fall of 1555, the distinguished bishops Nicholas Ridley and Hugh Latimer were burned at Oxford after refusing to submit. They were taken to the town ditch to be executed. As the flames rose about Latimer he uttered his last words, which became famous as a watchword for Protestant martyrs.

"Be of good cheer, Master Ridley," he called out to his companion, "and play the man; we shall this day light such a candle by God's grace in England as shall never be put out."

Rowland Taylor, a minister, was taken before Gardiner for preaching against the Catholic religion. The Chancellor called him a knave, traitor and heretic, and imprisoned him for nearly two years. When Taylor still refused to submit, he was taken to Aldham in Suffolk to be executed. He was an old man, and the crowd, seeing this saintly-looking cleric with his long white beard led to the stake, burst into tears. The sheriff then singled out a butcher and ordered, "Set up fagots."

The butcher wanted no part in the shameful business. "I am lame, sir, and unable to lift a fagot," he replied. They threatened him with imprisonment, but he still would not budge. At last they found three villainous scum of the village to bring up the bundles. One threw his load into Taylor's face, making it bleed. Another, who was drunk, struck the minister over the head with a halberd as the fire was lighted, a mercy because it killed Taylor and his body collapsed into the flames.

Burnings became a common sight over a large part of England, except for the strongly Catholic north. Many clergymen and others managed to flee into exile rather than give up their Protestant faith. And while some submitted, many others died the horrible death of "heretics" because they would not accept Catholicism. They included many of the common people. John Foxe, of Oxford University, collected histories of those who perished and published them in 1563 after Queen Mary's death in a famous volume commonly known as *Foxe's Book of Martyrs*.

In it Foxe told the stories of persons who were burned. The list includes such humble men as butchers, bricklayers, barbers, weavers, farmers, fullers, artisans and even housewives and maids, all of whom had the courage to face the flames rather than change their religion.

In May, 1556, a blind man, accused of heresy by a spiteful neighbor, and a cripple were brought before Edmund Bonner, Bishop of London. Both were condemned. After he was chained to the stake the cripple, Hugh Laverock, threw away his crutch and called out to his blind companion, "Be of good comfort, my brother, for my Lord of London is our good physician. He will heal us both shortly, thee of thy blindness and me of my lameness."

Almost all who died in the flames could have saved themselves by submitting. There was one notable exception, however: Thomas Cranmer. Since Cranmer, as Archbishop of Canterbury, had supported Henry VIII's Act of Supremacy, annulled the King's marriage to Catherine of Aragon and under Edward VI changed the Church of England over to its Protestant form, Mary imprisoned him in the Tower as soon as she became Queen.

With the approval of Rome, Cranmer was condemned to die. Having always been a pliable man, he wrote not one but six submissions to the Church of Rome, admitting his sins against it. But he reckoned without Mary's bitter hatred because he had degraded her mother by annulling the marriage to Henry VIII. The Queen approved Cranmer's execution.

They took him to Oxford to be burned. There he astonished those who expected to hear from him a final submission. Instead, he told them he repented having sinned by signing any.

At the stake, according to an eyewitness, Cranmer actually ran up the steps of the scaffold, and as the flames roared up, thrust his right hand, with which he had signed his submissions, into them, exclaiming, "This hand hath offended!"

The burnings went on, although there was much agitation

and disturbance against them. Before the terror subsided, over three hundred persons died at the stake.

Who was to blame? Chancellor Gardiner and Bishop Bonner handled or were responsible for most of the examinations and condemnations of the so-called heretics. Cardinal Pole, although he had steered England back to the Church of Rome, seems to have taken no part in the persecutions, although he apparently never opposed them. While Prince Philip was of course in favor of a wholly Catholic England, he does not appear to have had a part in the terror and was out of the kingdom during the last year or two. Yet Philip's influence over Mary was tremendous, and he may secretly have encouraged the persecutions.

Nevertheless, the greatest blame must rest upon Queen Mary. Some historians have exonerated her and said her name of "Bloody Mary" was not deserved. Yet she was Queen of England, the most powerful figure in the kingdom. She could have stopped the burnings by lifting her finger. She did not. In fact, three months before her death she rebuked the sheriff of Hampshire for reprieving a condemned man who had accepted Catholicism at the stake, and ordered the execution carried out, despite the fact that at the start of her reign she had promised that her subjects might worship according to their consciences.

Perhaps if Mary had seen one of the executions—for instance, the terrible one in April, 1556, when six men were burned together at Smithfield in a single fire—she might have changed her course.

Meanwhile, Mary convinced herself that her dearest wish was to be granted and she was to have a child. Many preparations were made for the great event, but by early August, 1555, the

Queen had to admit to herself that she had been mistaken. And with this discovery that no heir to the throne was to be born, Mary received another stunning blow. Prince Philip now felt sure she was too old to have a child, and decided to leave her.

He swore he would love Mary always; this trip to the Netherlands would last no more than a fortnight. He lied. The courtiers knew he did, and rumors spread among the people that the marriage was over. Only Mary clung desperately to the hope that they were wrong.

The Queen, to forget the tormenting thought that Philip had cast her off, plunged into the business of the kingdom. Yet she sat up late at night, writing impassioned letters to him. For a time he replied, but then his letters grew fewer and finally ceased.

Then came another blow. On November 12, 1555, Stephen Gardiner, as able a chancellor as the Queen could have found, whatever his sins in the religious persecutions, died. Mary made Nicholas Heath, Archbishop of York, her new Chancellor, and he was a far less able man than Gardiner.

Mary had one hope of persuading Philip to return. It appears that he was willing provided he would be crowned King. This hope vanished when Parliament refused to consider it; yet Mary continued to write her husband letters, sometimes humble and pleading, sometimes commanding him to come back, but in vain.

Still there was fear in England that Philip would return and be crowned. In 1556 a new conspiracy arose, led by a number of nobles and influential gentlemen. It was planned with the greatest care, so that it would not collapse like Wyatt's rebellion.

Money would be needed to pay and equip forces to carry out the plot. The daring plan was to get into the Exchequer and steal £50,000 stored there, a grant Parliament had made to Mary. The Tower was then to be seized and the Queen murdered. Meanwhile, Mary's onetime suitor, Edward Courtenay, who had fled to exile in France after Wyatt's rebellion, would invade England with an army of exiles and marry Princess Elizabeth, and the two would reign as King and Queen.

The plotters actually rehearsed the theft of the £50,000. Three of them were let into the Exchequer at night by a confederate in the building. There they weighed one of the chests containing the money and planned how to hoist them out to boats in the Thames, which flowed past the Exchequer.

As so often happened in such conspiracies, the plot was discovered by chance. A bricklayer, arrested on suspicion that he might be a traitor, was tortured and revealed something completely unexpected—a conversation he had heard about the conspiracy. The Council was then able to ferret out enough information to swoop down on the plotters.

Many were arrested and many executed; but although the conspiracy had been crushed in the nick of time, there was still so much unrest in England that the Queen lived in complete seclusion, surrounded by guards, in terror for her life.

Mary suspected that Princess Elizabeth might have been in the plot; in any event, being next in line for the throne, she was dangerous. However, the Queen was relieved of one other fear when Courtenay, who had remained in France and thus escaped the net in which the plotters in England were caught, fell ill and died.

Money was still a problem in spite of the grant Parliament had allowed the Queen. Economies were made. Loans were obtained from Antwerp moneylenders, and when these fell due the Queen demanded and got new loans from the great English trading company, the Merchant Adventurers, from the City of London and from wealthy landowners. Parliament refused to impose new taxes lest Mary use the money to help Philip and thus Spain, in its war with France.

Parliament had good reason to be worried about that, for in March, 1557, Philip suddenly returned to England. Poor, deluded Mary was delirious with joy, not realizing that Philip's only purpose was to drag England into the war with France. She obediently began to work on the Council, and while at first the members wanted no war, she managed to win them over. Preparations for war began. Ships and soldiers were sent to Calais, and on June 7, 1557, England declared war on France.

Now that Philip had successfully used Mary for his designs, he had no more need of her. He left England, this time for good. The Queen would never again see this conniving man who had treated her so cruelly.

The result of the war was disastrous. The defenses of Calais were weak, and after a week's siege it had to surrender to the French, who then took the surrounding area under English domination, called the Pale. Mary had lost the last bit of French soil England still held. She had lost a faithless husband who had never returned her passionate love. She had lost whatever respect and affection were left to her among her subjects, who were outraged over the loss of Calais. And while so many "heretics" had died at the stake, a powerful Protestant faction in England and in exile abroad remained to doom her plan to make the kingdom wholly Catholic once more.

Mercifully, the Queen's time on earth was short. Illnesses during the summer of 1558 that baffled her doctors caused the

Council to urge that she name Princess Elizabeth as her successor. At last Mary gave in, though she demanded that Elizabeth be asked to promise to continue the Catholic religion in England.

Envoys to Hatfield brought the news to Elizabeth, though there is no indication that she made the promise. Elizabeth meant to steer a very cautious course to avoid the religious rocks and shoals that might wreck her reign.

By November the Queen was very ill. She would lapse into unconsciousness for many hours, then rouse to tell her grieving ladies-in-waiting of her beautiful dreams, with little children in them singing like angels. This harsh, embittered woman had always loved children.

On November 17, 1558, Mary heard Mass very early in the morning. She was fully conscious, and able to make the responses, but a little later, before daybreak, she died.

Her life was a ruin. Everything she had set out to do had failed. She knew almost no happiness, and suffered much unjustly before coming to the throne. Her great plans had all come to nothing. She gave her heart to an ambitious adventurer who treated her shamefully. Mary had wanted to do good for England, but she did it only harm.

12

A Great Queen Begins Her Rule

TO BRING QUEEN ELIZABETH I back to life on paper is an impossible task, though many biographers have tried. The best one can do is to set down something of the strange and complex character of this daughter of Anne Boleyn, describe the important events of her reign and thus try to make real this woman who reunited England after the intrigue and confusion of Edward VI's reign and the horror of Mary's time, and played a large part in ending the greatest threat to England since William the Conqueror's invasion in 1066. She was feared, respected and loved by those close about her, and loved as no other English ruler by the common people of the kingdom.

Elizabeth was a maze of conflicting characteristics. She was self-confident, imperious and proud. She was given to furious fits of anger; the highest dukes and earls shriveled like dry leaves under her sarcasm and harsh criticism; her curses and bad language at times would put to shame those of the famous Billingsgate fishwives, whose vile speech has given us the word "billingsgate" to describe such talk.

Yet while she could send an enemy or traitor to imprisonment in the Tower, to the headsman's block on Tower Hill or to public hanging at Tyburn Tree by a word of command, she could be tender and merciful too. Elizabeth loved splendor and flattery, but she was wise, skeptical, watchful and cunning. Nothing pleased her more than to use her sharp wits at political intrigue, artful maneuvering, evasions and delays when it suited her purposes.

Elizabeth worked hard at the business of ruling England. She had the ability to play her part in the tough and ruthless art of politics that needed so much caution, intelligence and judgment. She ran her government at home and skillfully maintained relations and dealings with foreign nations.

Such was this last of the Tudors. She was twenty-five years old when Mary I died and the Council hurried to her residence at Hatfield to tell her she was Queen and to do her homage. She was not really beautiful; striking is perhaps a better word. She was of average height and fragile-looking, her skin so white that rather than pallor it had a beautiful glow, and her hair was a red-gold glory like that of her father. But it was her hands that would have interested a painter or sculptor—with their long, delicate and tapering fingers. Elizabeth's greatest beauty lay in her hands.

The new Queen did not wait for the usual formalities of going to London and taking possession of the Tower before making important appointments in her government and household. Among them were two destined to have a profound effect upon Elizabeth I's reign.

One, who came at once to Hatfield on a snow-white charger, was Lord Robert Dudley. He was exactly Elizabeth's age, and

142

they had known each other since childhood. He was tall, strikingly handsome, dark-haired and dark of complexion. There was a dark stain on his lineage too, for he was the son of the villainous John Dudley, Earl of Northumberland, and had been arrested in the Lady Jane Grey plot. Unlike his father, he did not go to the block. Although condemned to death, he was pardoned by Mary I. Dudley was married to an heiress, the former Amy Robsart. They had been wedded in 1550, when Dudley was seventeen. However, other love affairs lay lightly on his conscience; he was tired of Amy.

These defects in Lord Robert Dudley's ancestry and behavior made no difference to Queen Elizabeth. She appointed him Master of the Horse, in charge of all the royal horses. It was a higher post than it sounds, for it meant that he would be in close touch with the Queen. Soon Elizabeth would create him Earl of Leicester, the name by which he is famous. And he would become her lover for the rest of his life.

Although Elizabeth never married, lovers she had, and had to have, always, throughout her reign. Much has been written about whether she really wanted to marry at all. She knew she ought to in order to have an heir to succeed her, and she nearly did marry, more than once. But the evidence is strong that she never wanted a husband; the last thing in the world she would have stood for was a king-consort who might try to take some or all of the ruling power for himself. The most important thing in Elizabeth's life was to be Queen—and she wanted no interference with that.

Nevertheless, there were always her lovers. They had to make her believe that they had completely lost their heads over her (two actually *did* lose their heads—on the scaffold—though for betraying rather than loving her). But Elizabeth never for a moment lost hers. She used these suitors for her purposes, reveled in their adoration but never let her affection for them go too far.

The other important appointment Elizabeth made while she was still at Hatfield was her chief Secretary of State, Sir William Cecil, better known by the title the Queen bestowed on him in 1570, that of Lord Burghley. In 1558 he was thirty-eight, a quiet man with a long, spade-shaped face, able and a prodigiously hard worker. William Camden, the great English historian of Elizabeth's time, called him a genius.

They were entirely opposite in temperament. Sir William was like a brake on the racing motor of energy that was Queen Elizabeth I. But their aims were the same: to continue the Reformation, to keep England out of war and to put into effect a system of economy, as Elizabeth's grandfather, Henry VII, had done so successfully, so that England's credit would be high. Together they succeeded almost beyond belief at a time when costly wars in Europe were more common than peace, religious strife was rampant and most rulers were always seeking ways of paying off their debts. Elizabeth and Cecil, later Burghley, continued their association to the end of his life, five years before her own death. He was not one of her lovers, but he was more valuable than any she had.

Six days after becoming Queen, Elizabeth, with a great crowd of followers, set out for London and took possession of the Tower with the usual pomp and ceremony. As she arrived she spoke of how she had once been a prisoner there, only to rise to be Queen of the land. "Let me show myself to God thankful, and to men merciful," she said.

Elizabeth's coronation in Westminster Abbey on January 15, 1559, was the usual lavish procession from the Tower to Whitehall, then the gorgeous solemnity of the crowning. The most notable thing about it was the procession, for the Queen halted many times to let the people press forward to her chariot, where they could see this royal figure in her cloth of gold dress and mantle and ermine cape, the radiance of her hair and the alabaster, oval face with its almost invisible pale eyebrows. She smiled at them, and they fell in love with her. It was the beginning of Elizabeth's greatest and most important love affair—that with her people.

Elizabeth called her first Parliament on January 25. The most pressing question they faced was that of religion. Mary I had torn England apart by her anti-Protestant measures; the kingdom might easily remain so if stern anti-Catholic laws were passed.

The strongly Protestant House of Commons passed a new Act of Supremacy, once more abolishing the power of the Pope in England, though in a form much less offensive to Catholics. And a little later the extreme Protestant doctrines of Edward VI's reign were eased by the adoption of a new set of rules, the Thirty-Nine Articles. Nevertheless, all Catholic bishops and about two hundred Catholic clergy were ousted.

Elizabeth did her best to bring about religious peace in England. Yet there was still much conflict. The Catholics rejected the new Act of Supremacy, while the strict Puritans, growing more powerful daily, demanded sterner measures against the Catholics.

In Rome, Pope Pius V, an austere, aggressive man, struck back by excommunicating the Queen and releasing all English Catholics from allegiance to her. Elizabeth retaliated when the Treason Act was passed in 1571. For anyone writing, preaching or speaking of the Queen as a heretic or a usurper of the English crown, the penalty was death. And between 1571 and 1585 twenty-one persons, eighteen of them priests, were executed under this law.

Yet there was never any religious strife under Elizabeth that approached the horrors of Mary's reign. Her first Archbishop of Canterbury, Matthew Parker, did much to preserve at least a degree of religious peace in the kingdom.

Another matter of consequence came up to trouble Elizabeth only a few days after her coronation, and it continued to vex her through a large part of her reign. On February 6, 1559, a delegation from Parliament and the Council called on her at Whitehall Palace.

"We humbly urge you, your Majesty, to give thought to a suitable marriage, in order that the succession to the crown through your heir may be assured," its leader said.

Elizabeth gave them a long and gracious reply. In the course of it she said she would do as God directed her, adding, "If He directs me not to marry, He will surely provide for the succession in other ways." She took off her coronation ring and held it up for them to see. "I am already bound unto a husband, which is the Kingdom of England."

Nevertheless, there were plenty of suitors. Most important of them was Philip II of Spain, widower of Mary I. Philip was anxious to marry Elizabeth, but she told his emissary plainly that she did not wish to marry. She realized, she said, that their marriage would unite their kingdoms in friendship and against the ever-present danger to both countries from France, but she hinted of her doubts about marrying her half-sister's former husband.

Her father, Henry VIII, had caused himself great trouble by marrying his brother Prince Arthur's widow, Catherine of Aragon.

There were more—Prince Eric of Sweden, the Duke of Saxony, Archduke Charles of Austria, the Scottish Earl of Arran and other foreign royalty and nobility. Parliament and the Council would have preferred to have Elizabeth marry an Englishman, and there was no lack of suitors at home, either. None pleased Elizabeth except one, and in that case marriage seemed impossible. He was Robert Dudley, later to be Earl of Leicester.

In 1560, Dudley was the man closest to the Queen in England, her favorite and in love with her. Elizabeth spent much time with him; in fact, the dedicated, far-seeing Cecil begged the Spanish ambassador, who had influence with the Queen, to speak to her about it.

"In God's name, my Lord," Cecil said, "point out to her the effect of her intimacy with this man. He is thinking of killing his wife, since she is said to be ill. She is perfectly well, and aware that she must use care not to be poisoned."

Probably it was on that same day, September 8, 1560, that Amy Robsart Dudley was found dead of a broken neck at the foot of the stairway in her house. An investigation determined that her death was accidental. It was more likely suicide, but the rumor mongers were sure that Dudley had killed her so he could marry Elizabeth.

The Queen, as she so often did, changed her mind about Dudley several times. First she proclaimed him completely innocent. It was even rumored that they were secretly married. Then, after appointing him a peer, she cut the document in two with a knife. Later she did create him Earl of Leicester for political

147

reasons, and he remained her close adviser for the rest of his life.

Only one other man came close to marrying her—the Duke of Alençon, a member of the French royal family. This was a strange attraction, for the duke was practically a dwarf, his face badly scarred by smallpox and his nose enormous. Not only that, but Alençon had the effrontery to send a representative, Jean de Simier, to court the Queen. He did it so successfully that the Queen was swept off her feet by her "Monkey," as she nicknamed this suitor by proxy for Alençon.

Later, when Alençon himself arrived, Elizabeth was attracted in spite of the duke's odd appearance. He was twenty-three and Elizabeth forty-six. This would undoubtedly be the Queen's last chance of bearing an heir to the throne, if it were not too late already. As usual, she could not make up her mind. She loved Alençon one day; the next she did not. Yet she might have married him but for the horror of the Puritans over a Catholic husband. And at last she sent her "Frog," as she called him, back to France.

Not that all of Elizabeth's time was taken up in dallying with her favorite suitors. Far from it. She kept constantly in close touch with her ministers, discussing foreign affairs and those at home, and using her almost miraculous talent for diplomacy, intrigue and administration. Nor did she forget the people of England, whom she loved as they loved her. She took care of that on her progresses.

Elizabeth made many of them, usually each summer, since the best of the English roads were bad enough in those months, almost impassable quagmires in the wet seasons and out of the question for a queen to travel in winter. There are those who say she made them with a third purpose beyond exhibiting herself to her people and getting to know her kingdom—that, being like her grandfather, Henry VII, she used her progresses to save herself money.

It is true that she expected and received the most costly and lavish entertainment at the houses of the nobles she visited. But it must be remembered that there were many other expenses connected with a progress that the Queen had to pay herself— the transportation and feeding of at least five hundred courtiers and servants who went along, and the many tents and pavilions taken in case the progress had to halt in wilderness overnight or have a roadside picnic lunch. And when Elizabeth was not on progress, the courtiers lived in whatever palace she fancied, with all their expenses paid.

However, Elizabeth was entertained at great cost wherever she went. Often enough some noble or prelate selected for the honor of a visit on progress faced ruin because of the tremendous expense. These unfortunate ones invented all sorts of reasons to keep the Queen from coming. Most were too proud to admit that they could not afford it. Some would say their house was too small to accommodate the Queen in proper style. Sometimes they said the plague had struck their neighborhoods. Others intrigued with the officials who planned the Queen's itinerary to steer her away from their manors, or at least to make the visit a short one. Even Elizabeth's first Archbishop of Canterbury, Matthew Parker, artfully suggested that the Queen might prefer to stay in her own more luxurious palace when she reached Canterbury.

Probably the most lavish entertainment ever provided for the Queen on a progress was in the summer of 1575 at her favorite Leicester's famous Kenilworth Castle in Warwickshire. This three-week visit of the Queen almost defies description. Preparations were made for weeks ahead, and Leicester met Elizabeth seven miles away, where a feast was held in a tent so large that it took seven carts to haul it away afterwards.

In the magnificent castle, which Elizabeth had given Leicester, no expense had been spared in furnishing it with costly accommodations for her Majesty. A cannon salute welcomed her, and the great clock on one of the towers was stopped, for time was to stand still as long as the Queen remained. At night the castle grounds were a fairyland of light from candles and torches. There were tremendous displays of fireworks, hunting parties, brilliantly lighted evening water pageants on the castle pool, sports and plays presented by the country people and indescribably rich banquets. What all this cost Leicester can only be imagined, but even the Archbishop of Canterbury's much more modest entertainment cost him £2,000—a vast sum in those days.

On the whole, things went smoothly with Elizabeth I until 1568, nine years after she had become Queen. Then something happened that was to trouble her for nineteen years afterward. Elizabeth had been concerned for two years before 1568 by the stormy career of her cousin, Mary Queen of Scots, next in line for the English throne, but it was not until that year that Mary Stuart became the most worrisome problem of the reign until 1587.

13

Mary Queen of Scots

TWO QUEENS. THEY WERE COUSINS OF SORTS, both descended from Henry VII. They wrote many letters to each other, yet they never met. Most of the letters were filled with endearments, but the two were rivals if not actual enemies—one sitting on the throne of England, the other Queen of Scotland. For centuries the two countries had shed each other's blood by the bucketful in wars and border raids.

Mary Stuart was very different from Elizabeth. She had spent her girlhood and young womanhood in France, brought up in the soft luxury and extravagance of the French Court. She had almost no skill in governing a nation, diplomacy or political intrigue, and was pitifully weak. Her life is a fantastic story, filled with romance, intrigue, rebellion, fighting and two frightful murders.

Princess Elizabeth was nine years old when Mary Stuart was born on December 8, 1542, becoming Queen of Scots just six days later when her father, James V of Scotland, died. Henry VIII tried in vain to betroth the infant Queen Mary to his son

Edward, five years older, and thus make possible the union of those ancient enemies, England and Scotland. When the Scots spurned his offer, he tried what he called "rough wooing"—a murderous series of raids in which Edinburgh was burned, its royal palace of Holyrood sacked and the surrounding countryside laid waste. During that time the baby Queen of Scots was hidden from the English enemy until she was finally spirited away to France, the native land of her mother, Mary of Guise, widow of James V, who remained in Scotland as regent while her daughter grew up.

When Elizabeth was twenty-four and her half-sister Mary I ruled England, the fifteen-year-old Mary Queen of Scots was married to Prince Francis of France, and a year later became a Queen of France as well as Scotland when Henry II of France died and Francis was King. Less than two years later young Francis II died, and Mary Stuart returned to rule Scotland. Elizabeth was then Queen of England. Mary Queen of Scots would be heir to the throne of England if she, Elizabeth, died without children. Elizabeth was twenty-seven, unmarried and not likely to marry.

News came to London that Mary Queen of Scots was in trouble. Her half-brother James, whom Mary had created Earl of Moray and who was the real ruler of Scotland, was determined to make the country, like England, fully Protestant. But Mary Stuart was as strong a Catholic as Mary I of England had been. She might not only defeat Moray's plans and make Scotland Catholic, but do the same for England if she were ever to rule there too. From then on, Queen Elizabeth watched her cousin closely.

More disturbing news reached England. It was said that Mary Stuart was going to marry Lord Henry Darnley. Elizabeth was well acquainted with this boy, whose pretty golden head must have been filled with straw, for he certainly had no brains inside it. Darnley's father had been exiled from Scotland, and the boy had been born and lived in England until recently. Elizabeth sent an emissary north to dissuade Mary Stuart from marrying Darnley, but Mary was head over heels in love with the girlishly handsome young man. They were married on July 29, 1565.

The Earl of Moray asked Elizabeth to help him start a revolt and overthrow the Queen of Scots. She promised to send Moray troops, but as so often happened in her reign, she unexplainably changed her mind. When Moray went ahead with the revolt, Mary Stuart's men crushed it and the earl fled to England, where Elizabeth gave him a tongue-lashing for not knowing better than to start the revolt in the first place. When Elizabeth broke a promise, she always blamed the other person.

Elizabeth got reports from her spies of everything that went on in other capitals of Europe. First she heard of how passionately Mary Stuart loved Darnley, and that she was ready to let him have all the power he wanted. Then came word that the romance was no longer flourishing. The imbecilic Darnley, being godlike in looks, had, it seemed, come to believe he *was* a god of sorts. Arrogant, rude and loud-spoken, he was trying to play the dictator with the Scottish Council. He was drinking too much; the English Court heard that he had turned on his wife in a drunken rage at a social affair and berated her shamefully.

The gossip from Scotland kept filtering through, and most of it rang true. Mary Stuart had refused her husband's demand that she give him equal authority in the government. She had turned against him completely. Darnley, the stories went, was furious and bent on revenge.

He got it. London gasped when it heard how, although the Court was already buzzing with tales about David Riccio, a handsome Italian singer and musician who had become Mary Stuart's favorite and private secretary, while she no longer had anything to do with Darnley.

As had happened before, Riccio was dining with the Queen and a small party on the evening of March 9, 1566, at Holyrood Palace when Darnley burst in, followed by six cutthroats. The ruffians seized Riccio, dragged him screaming for help into a turret of the palace, stabbed him more than fifty times with daggers and left him dead in a pool of blood.

More stunning news followed. Mary Stuart, it seemed, had forgiven her husband for his part in the murder. The English Court couldn't understand it. Darnley had turned against the rest of the conspirators, and he and Mary put down a revolt they started—an attempt to seize the Scottish throne.

For a time after that things seemed to be peaceful in Scotland. London heard of the birth of a son and heir to the Scottish throne to Mary Stuart and Darnley at Stirling Castle on June 19, 1566.

Then new rumors reached the English capital that made many noblemen who knew James Hepburn, Earl of Bothwell, shake their heads. Bothwell, they knew, was a murderous ruffian, though in spite of his evil reputation, this tall, broadshouldered man had a fatal attraction for women. Mary Queen of Scots had fallen so madly in love with Bothwell that she had lost all sense of right or wrong and any concern for her kingdom or even for her fate.

Most people in Queen Elizabeth's Court thought Mary Stuart's infatuation with Bothwell would come to nothing. Even if Catholic Mary could overcome the near impossibility of a divorce from Catholic Darnley, their little son's right to succeed to the Scottish crown would be endangered.

But in February, 1567, came truly staggering news. At two o'clock on the morning of February 10 a house called Kirk o' Field, just outside the walls of Edinburgh, had been blown sky-high by a charge of gunpowder. Beyond the rubble that had once been the house, in its garden, searchers found Darnley's body. He had not been killed in the explosion. He had been strangled.

Gradually, more details of the shocking murder reached London. It was believed certain that Bothwell had been responsible for Darnley's death. Darnley, apparently suspecting Bothwell's intentions, had gone to his father's house in Glasgow, where he would be safer than in Edinburgh. There he had fallen seriously ill. As soon as he had recovered enough to travel, Mary Stuart had gone to Glasgow and persuaded him to come back to Edinburgh with her.

Why had he gone to Kirk o' Field? Why not the more comfortable Holyrood Palace or the safer, formidable Edinburgh Castle? Some reports had it that Darnley had chosen Kirk o' Field himself because the air would be purer for his convalescence. Most people snorted over that. It just didn't ring true.

There was another odd thing about the Kirk o' Field tragedy. A few hours before the explosion, Queen Mary had been dining there with her husband and a few friends. About eleven o'clock she suddenly remembered she had promised to take part in the wedding festivities for her favorite valet at Holyrood Palace. So the party at Kirk o' Field had broken up.

Most Londoners were convinced that Mary Queen of Scots was implicated in the plot to kill Darnley. She undoubtedly had not been among those who had strangled her husband, but the affair made her a bloody-handed murderess just the same. Nor was this the end of it. Although reports indicated that Mary Stuart was doing nothing to bring her husband's murderers to justice, Darnley's father, the Earl of Lennox, charged that Bothwell was the leader of the assassins.

Bothwell was arrested and brought to trial in Edinburgh's grim prison and town hall, the Tolbooth. He swaggered into the courtroom fearlessly, since four thousand of his supporters were in Edinburgh and his only accuser, Darnley's father, did not dare come to the city. Bothwell was quickly acquitted and swaggered out again.

He and Mary Queen of Scots were married in the chapel of Holyrood on May 15, 1567. Bothwell was now the real ruler of Scotland, since the infatuated Mary let him do exactly as he pleased.

More events in the loathsome drama unfolded. A group of Scottish lords marched against Bothwell, whose own army melted away when his supporters saw they were facing better-trained and -equipped enemies. Mary Queen of Scots remained loyally at Bothwell's side, but he deserted her and galloped away. He was outlawed and finally reached Denmark, where he was to die, insane, ten years later.

Elizabeth should have been easier in her mind when the rebel Scottish lords imprisoned Mary in a lonely castle in Loch Leven. Yet she wrote Mary, criticizing her harshly for the Bothwell affair, but also sent her captors a letter saying she would declare war on Scotland if they used any violence against her cousin.

Why Elizabeth did this in behalf of the woman she feared most in the world was one of the strange moves that so often took place in her reign.

Elizabeth's threat against the rebel lords sobered them, but a great stroke of luck came their way with the discovery of the famous Casket Letters between Mary and Bothwell. There is much disagreement among historians as to whether the letters were genuine or forgeries, but they gave Mary's captors exactly what they needed, for they incriminated her in Darnley's murder. The lords confronted her with the letters and demanded that she resign her crown.

"No!" cried the Queen. "I will not sign! I will forfeit my life rather than my crown!"

"You had better sign," threatened one of the scowling lords, "or you will force us to cut your throat." At last Mary abdicated, though as she signed she did not, in her own mind, yield her right to the Scottish crown.

The English government learned, of course, that she had been forced to abdicate, but until May, 1568, it was known only that she was still a prisoner. In that month Queen Elizabeth received a pathetic letter from her cousin, imploring for help and asylum in England. Mary Stuart was already there, for she had written from the little northwestern English seaport of Workington in Cumberland. She had tried once and failed to escape from her island prison, but a second attempt had succeeded.

Elizabeth pitied her cousin and wanted her to live at Court, but Cecil, a strict Protestant, hated her. He was sure Mary had had a part in Darnley's murder and convinced Elizabeth that in England this ardent Catholic would be a menace to the kingdom.

Mary Stuart went to Carlisle, the shire town of Cumberland.

157

There Sir Francis Knollys, a seasoned diplomat, met and made her welcome in England. Then he came to the real reason for his mission. "It is her Majesty the Queen's pleasure, Madam, that you must be purged of the stain of your husband's murder before she receives you at Court. This can be done only if you submit yourself to the judgment of her Majesty."

Mary was willing, but then she received a letter from her cousin making it plain that she would have to appear before investigators appointed by Elizabeth, and this, as a queen, Mary refused to do at first. However, Elizabeth added: "And I promise on the word of a prince [meaning a ruler], that no persuasion of your subjects or advice of others shall ever induce me to move you to anything dangerous to you or your honor."

How well Elizabeth kept this promise will soon be seen.

Knollys finally persuaded Mary Stuart to appear before Elizabeth's commissioners, as well as a group of her enemies in Scotland headed by her kinsman the Earl of Moray. She was confronted with the Casket Letters, and Moray charged her with having been instrumental in Darnley's murder. Mary stood on her rights as a queen and refused to answer. At last Elizabeth ended the investigation, saying that the charges were not sufficiently proved.

Now what was she to do with her troublesome cousin? With the stain of murder still hanging over Mary's head, she could scarcely appear at Court. But if Elizabeth let Mary go free she might raise a Spanish or French army abroad, invade Scotland, regain her crown and perhaps even rule England as a Catholic queen. Mary I had proved how frightful that could be.

The best thing, Elizabeth decided, was to keep Mary Stuart in England, well guarded. So Mary was sent to Tutbury Castle in Staffordshire. She had her own household, with her expenses paid, along with her pension from France as its Dowager Queen and a good deal of freedom, though never a chance to escape. For nineteen years Mary Stuart remained in "honorable custody" —a prisoner yet not a prisoner. From time to time she was transferred from one castle to another. She generally lived in comfort and could ride, hunt and play outdoor games.

Twice in those nineteen years, Mary Stuart was active in plots against Elizabeth. The first was the result of the efforts of Thomas Howard, Duke of Norfolk, to marry her. Mary was not unwilling, but Norfolk began a dangerous, rash conspiracy for the invasion of England by a Spanish army, aided by an uprising of English Catholics. Elizabeth was to be seized and Mary and Norfolk take the throne in her place.

How much Mary had to do with this scheme is not definitely known. But the English government learned of the plot. Norfolk was arrested, tried for treason and executed on Tower Hill in June, 1572. It was the first time in the fourteen years of Elizabeth's reign that she had signed a death warrant for the beheading of a noble. There was a great outcry from the people for Mary Stuart's execution too, but Elizabeth, perhaps thinking of the solemn promise she had given Mary, would not approve it.

For the next ten years Mary Stuart continued to live quietly in her "honorable custody." But all the while she was corresponding secretly with friends in the hope that an invasion of England would come. In 1582 such a plan developed. An invasion was to be led by Mary's French uncle, the Duke of Guise, with money supplied by Philip II of Spain. Again, news of the plot leaked out. A conspirator was arrested and under torture revealed a mass of evidence showing that Mary Stuart at least knew of the plot.

Measures were immediately taken to shut off Mary's communication with the outside world, but Sir Francis Walsingham,

Elizabeth's Secretary of State and long the master spy of all the Queen's secret agents, wanted Mary moved to a place where she could continue her secret correspondence, which could then be intercepted and decoded.

Mary was transferred to Chartley Manor in Derbyshire. Like the fly in the nursery rhyme, she walked straight into the web the spider, Walsingham, had spun. She began sending out letters in beer barrels and receiving replies in the same way.

By May, 1586, Walsingham had details of a sinister new plot. Spanish troops were to invade England. At the same time, Antony Babington, a rich young Catholic who was in love with Mary Stuart, would rescue her from Chartley. Meanwhile, six English rebels at the English Court would either stab or shoot Queen Elizabeth.

In August, Walsingham pounced. Fourteen conspirators were arrested. All were condemned to death, seven by the most horrible way known in England. They were hanged, cut down while still alive and slit open, their hearts and intestines ripped out before their dying eyes and their bodies then quartered.

Meanwhile, Mary Stuart, blissfully unaware that she had been caught in treason, was suddenly confronted by a group of horsemen during a hunting party. Their leader dismounted and said to Mary, "Madam, the Queen, my mistress, finds it very strange that you . . . should have conspired against her and her State. . . ."

Mary, stunned with surprise, stammered, "My Lord, I have always shown myself a good sister and friend to her Majesty."

Her protest fell on deaf ears. She was arrested and taken to the manor of Tixhall. Meanwhile, her quarters at Chartley were searched and many incriminating letters seized.

On September 21, 1586, Mary was taken to the gloomy, brooding castle of Fotheringhay in Northamptonshire, used as a state prison. A commission of twenty-four peers and Privy Councillors was appointed to try her for treason.

Under the conditions of her trial, Mary was allowed no counsel to defend her and no witnesses to testify in her behalf. And while this was in accordance with the law, there was no justification for trying her for treason against the Crown, since she was not an English subject.

This difficulty had to be circumvented somehow, as Elizabeth well knew. She tossed the problem into the laps of the English lawyers. They came up with the fact that in feudal times England had claimed sovereignty over Scotland, so Mary Stuart was an English subject. This dusty claim did not satisfy Elizabeth. The Queen wrote a letter, handed to Mary Stuart at her trial: the proceedings were legal, said Elizabeth, since Mary, being in England, was subject to English law.

To this, Mary replied calmly, "I came to England on my cousin's promise of assistance against my enemies and rebel subjects, and was at once imprisoned. I do not recognize the laws of England. . . ."

It had not been at all certain that Mary would even appear at the trial, which she knew would be a mockery. Elizabeth then held out the bait of possible mercy in another letter in which she charged Mary with conspiring against her life. But she added, "Answer fully, and you may receive greater favor from us."

Mary seems to have trusted in this hint of mercy. Perhaps she thought that now Elizabeth would honor her solemn promise that no harm should come to Mary in England. She appeared at her trial in Fotheringhay Castle elegantly dressed in black velvet with a white headdress and veil. She was so lame from rheumatism and lack of exercise that she had to be supported as she limped in.

After explaining to Mary that she was on trial for planning to overthrow Elizabeth, the Lord Chamberlain concluded, "You are to have every opportunity to declare your innocence."

Declare her innocence Mary Stuart did, but it had little weight against the evidence that was piled up against her. Soon the trial was transferred to the Star Chamber in Westminster. Elizabeth ordered it; she wanted no sentence passed until she had gone over the proceedings.

When the Court reconvened, it found Mary Stuart guilty of contriving "matters tending to the death and destruction of the Queen of England." The penalty, of course, was death—unless Elizabeth kept the promise made so long ago and pardoned Mary.

Elizabeth was not pleased with the trial. She had wanted a confession of guilt from Mary. Under her orders to wring one from the condemned Queen of Scots, Mary's jailer tried, but failed utterly.

Meanwhile, Elizabeth was suffering torments of indecision. She did not want to confirm Mary's death sentence in spite of demands from Parliament that she do so.

As far as Mary Stuart could tell, however, death was drawing near. Her guard at Fotheringhay had been strengthened. Mary herself wrote Elizabeth a farewell letter. Some of the words must have burned themselves into Elizabeth's agitated brain: ". . . On the eve of leaving this world and preparing myself for a better one, I remind you that one day you will have to answer for your charge. . . ."

Still the days passed and nothing happened. At last, however,

Elizabeth was forced to act. She used a transparent pretext in doing so. The secretary of the Council was ordered to bring the long-unsigned death warrant to the Queen. He was to put it among a pile of other papers ready for Elizabeth's signature.

The Queen acted as if nothing unusual was afoot. "A beautiful winter morning," she remarked, and then asked, "What are those papers on the table?"

"Instruments for your Majesty's signature," replied the secretary, following orders.

With that, the Queen hurriedly scratched "Elizabeth R" ("R" for Regina, or Queen) on all the papers without reading them. Her next words betrayed her, however: "Have the Great Seal attached to the warrant and take it to Walsingham." She added a grim joke about the man who had hounded Mary Stuart to her doom: "I fear the grief thereof will go near to kill him outright."

Now that the death warrant was signed, guilt was heavy on Elizabeth's conscience. Besides, there would be the anger of France and Scotland to be reckoned with.

As the secretary was leaving, she called him back. "Is there no way to save me from the embarrassment of this affair?" she murmured. "If some loyal subject were to do the deed aforehand— let Walsingham write Sir Amyas Paulet of the matter. . . ."

If someone murdered Mary Stuart before her execution, Elizabeth's hands would be clean. But even the Queen's dread vengeance on those who offended her could not keep Paulet, Mary's jailer at Fotheringhay, from writing an indignant refusal "to shed blood without law or warrant."

The Queen ranted furiously against Paulet, but preparations were already complete for Mary Stuart's execution. After dinner on February 7, Mary received the news that she was to die the next morning. She heard her fate calmly, and asked only that her Catholic chaplain be with her and that she be given more time to prepare for death. Both requests were refused.

Between eight and nine the next morning, February 8, 1587, Mary Queen of Scots entered the great hall of Fotheringhay. Before her was a wooden stage two feet high and twelve feet square, draped in black cloth. On it were two stools for the official witnesses, the Earls of Shrewsbury and Kent. Beside them stood the block, about two feet high, with a little stool for Mary to sit on while she was being disrobed. Nearby lay the great sharp ax.

As Mary came in, the spectators, largely nobility, saw a tall, regal woman dressed in black save for a white peaked headdress setting off the auburn hair beneath it, and a long white veil down her back.

On the stage, when the death warrant had been read, the Protestant dean of Peterborough began to preach to Mary. "Mr. Dean," the Queen of Scots said firmly, "I am settled in the ancient Catholic Roman religion, and mind to spend my blood in defense of it."

The dean knelt on the scaffold steps and began to pray, but Mary ignored him, fell to her knees and prayed, first in Latin and then in English. As she finished, the executioner and his assistant, masked and robed in black with white aprons, asked and received her pardon for what they were about to do. Then, as Mary's outer dress was removed, the spectators gasped. Her petticoat, bodice and sleeves were all red—the color of blood and in the Catholic Church the color of martyrdom. Mary was playing the last act of her life's drama perfectly.

"Do not mourn," the Queen of Scots consoled her two weeping ladies, "but rather rejoice." One of them put the white blindfold, embroidered in gold, over her eyes, and they left the stage.

Mary knelt on the cushion before the block, reciting a psalm in Latin. She felt for the block, put her head on it and in Latin said, "Into Your hands, O Lord, I commend my spirit."

The executioner bungled his first stroke, which merely cut the back of her head. With the second, her head was severed.

Then came a dreadful spectacle. The executioner picked up Mary Stuart's head and held it aloft, crying, "God save the Queen!" Suddenly it slipped from his hand, leaving only an auburn wig in his grasp. As the head rolled on the floor, the horrified people saw that the forty-four-year-old Mary's own hair was gray and scanty. The privations of her long captivity had left her an old woman.

Elizabeth I also put on a dramatic act at Greenwich Palace when the news reached her. She was first indignant, then in terrible distress, weeping constantly. Next came the dreaded fit of anger. She had the wretched secretary of the Council thrown into the Tower for daring to carry out her command about the death warrant. She questioned the members of the Council as if they had been criminals. How could this terrible thing have been done when she, Elizabeth the Queen, had had no intention of executing Mary?

It was only when the courageous Cecil told her bluntly that she was deceiving no one that she subsided, pardoned the Council and released the innocent secretary from the Tower, though she fined him £10,000 for his "criminal" actions.

Thus was Elizabeth rid of a menace to her throne. But a still greater one was in the making in Spain. There, Philip II was about to put into action his dream of conquering England and making it a part of his empire.

14

The Armada and the
Tudors' Sunset

THE SPANIARDS CALLED IT Enterprise of England; it is better
known, of course, as the Spanish Armada. Not only Philip's
ambition drove him to plan the Enterprise. He had a score to
settle with Sir Francis Drake. Drake was one of the great men
Elizabeth I had to make her reign glorious. The Spanish called
him a pirate, and they had reason to. Beyond that, he was a true
sailor, an adventurer and a great sea fighter.

In 1572, when England and Spain were officially at peace,
Drake took his own ship to the New World, raided and burned
Spanish colonies in Mexico and Central America, captured Spanish ships and brought back booty of £40,000 in coin. Next he
sailed around the world from 1577 to 1580 with five ships, re-
turning with his flagship, the *Golden Hind,* and the others
stuffed with gold, silver, jewels, spices and silks. Those who in-
vested in the venture, including Elizabeth herself, got a return of
4,700 per cent on their money. As a result, the Queen knighted
Drake.

The Spaniards were furious. They had always regarded the

Pacific as their own private ocean. They complained bitterly of Drake's piracy there and demanded the return of the money. Queen Elizabeth found herself unable to oblige Philip II. She was very fond of money.

Spain now began preparations in earnest for the Enterprise. Sir Francis offered to raid the coast of Spain and destroy as many as possible of the ships Philip was gathering there. It might not stop the Enterprise, but it could delay it, perhaps for a year, giving England time she desperately needed to prepare her navy and land defenses.

Elizabeth gave Sir Francis four great galleons with two decks fitted with heavy cannon to fire smashing, ship-sinking broadsides, along with towering forecastles and sterncastles at each end, mounted with smaller, faster-firing guns. The Queen also provided two pinnaces, small, fast, low-built craft that could be sailed or rowed. Drake had four fighting ships of his own. London merchants were to furnish as many more ships as possible.

Drake gathered his vessels at Plymouth, working like a demon to put them in shape and equip them for the voyage. On April 2, 1587, he was ready to sail.

Then, as was almost certain to happen when she had a hand in any project, Elizabeth changed her mind. She sent a horseman galloping at breakneck speed for Plymouth to stop Drake. Fortunately, when the rider arrived, the sails of Drake's twenty-five or so vessels had disappeared over the horizon.

Drake headed straight for Cadiz. There he drove off a squadron of small Spanish galleys, formidable but no match for heavy warships, burned thirty or more ships anchored in the harbor and sailed away before the Spaniards could bring in a stronger fighting force.

Drake's ships captured many small coastwise vessels off the southern coast of Portugal, then ruled by Spain. Most were loaded with hoops and staves for the big barrels called pipes used in that wine-producing region. Drake had them all burned. He knew exactly what he was doing, for, as we shall see, the destruction of those hoops and staves was of more value to the English than the burning of the ships at Cadiz.

Homeward bound, Drake veered off his course for the Azores, almost as though he had smelled out the Portuguese carrack *San Felipe*, which was sailing from Goa with a cargo worth about £114,000. She surrendered, and Drake then headed for England with the booty.

As he left Cadiz, Drake had said, "I have singed the King's beard." A portrait of Sir Francis shows him as a rather small man with a decisive mouth and eyes, dark hair, thin mustache and small beard. He has a quizzical look that hints strongly of Drake's mischievous satisfaction at having "singed the King's beard."

The chess board where this game on which the fate of England depended was being plotted included Spain and Portugal, the English Channel, the Low Countries across the North Sea from England and the southern and southeastern coasts of England itself.

The Spanish plan envisioned assembling at Lisbon the most powerful fleet the world had ever seen and sailing into the English Channel to meet, fight, defeat and if possible destroy the English fleet. Next would come the chief purpose of the Enterprise—invasion.

The Low Countries were then in revolt against domination by Spain. One of the great generals of his time, Alexander Farnese, Duke of Parma, was putting the rebellion down with an army of 30,000 men. He now had things well under control; thus, off Dunkirk, then part of Flanders, his army, in barges, would be escorted across the North Sea by the victorious Armada, go ashore and overwhelm England.

Ill luck for the Enterprise began early. On February 9, 1588, the Spanish commanding admiral, the Marquis of Santa Cruz, veteran of a score of victorious sea fights, died. With him went Spain's best hope of victory in the English Channel.

Philip II then named the Duke of Medina Sidonia to command the Armada as "Captain General of the Ocean Sea." A mild, gentle man, intelligent and able, Medina Sidonia was no sea dog. The few times he had been at sea he had been seasick the whole voyage. He did not want the job, but he obeyed Philip II's command.

Medina Sidonia did an excellent job of fitting out the Armada for sea. At Lisbon, Santa Cruz had already assembled thirteen galleons; four large warships called galleasses that cruised under sail, used oars in battle and mounted fifty guns apiece, some of large size; and sixty or seventy other ships of every kind, many slow, others leaky, all short of proper armament and some crank —so poorly built that they might break in half or capsize in a storm. Medina Sidonia found some of the vessels overloaded, some almost empty, some with too many guns and some with very few and some with no cannonballs.

The new admiral efficiently put things in proper shape. Then, needing more guns, he obtained about seventy, most of them probably of iron and of small size. The culverins he wanted— long brass cannon that could hurl heavy balls at long range and cripple an enemy—and the smaller but also effective brass demi-culverins were hard to come by. Master gunsmiths were scarce, casting a good cannon took time and these big guns were very costly.

Nevertheless, as spring came, Medina Sidonia had obtained some extra-heavy guns. He had twenty galleons, including eight fine big ones, one of them his flagship, the *Florencia*. He also had forty armed merchantmen. Many more ships followed these. By the end of April, the Captain General of the Ocean Sea had about 130 vessels in fair condition for sea. They carried 8,000 sailors and 20,000 soldiers to join Parma's army. His supply of powder had almost doubled since he had reached Lisbon. Every ship had enough cannonballs for each gun to fire fifty rounds.

Yet Medina Sidonia had troubles. The ships had been kept fully manned since the Armada had begun to assemble in October, 1587. Replacement of provisions had been expensive. Money to pay the soldiers and sailors had not arrived, and many men had deserted. The Armada had neither a full complement of trained gunners nor enough big cannon.

The Armada sailed from Lisbon on May 9, 1588. Medina Sidonia felt confident; plans for the sea fight, the rendezvous with Parma and the invasion were complete to the last detail. Progress was slow, however, since the fleet could move no faster than the slowest old hulks trailing astern of the warships. It took them thirteen days to sail a little over 160 sea miles northward.

Then, as warmer weather set in, Drake's wise destruction of the captured, seasoned barrel staves and hoops paid off richly for the English. The new food and water casks that had had to be made were mostly of green wood, which swelled and leaked. Cask after cask of food was found to be spoiled. Water butt after water butt contained only a little green, slimy liquid.

170

They put into the far northern Spanish port of Corunna to repair the leaky bottoms of the older ships, take on water and locate what fresh provisions they could. That took a month. And the leaky casks were still giving trouble, as they would all through the expedition. But at last, on July 30, the Armada sighted the point in Cornwall called the Lizard, at the entrance to the English Channel.

Meanwhile, Elizabeth had sought by negotiations to keep peace. War meant the interruption of England's enormously profitable woolen trade, which was why the Queen had tried to keep Drake from singeing King Philip's beard.

Yet in December, 1587, when it was reported that Santa Cruz might sail from Lisbon before Christmas, Elizabeth acted swiftly. In a fortnight the fleet was manned and ready for sea. Along the coasts and inland, a chain of beacons stalked over the downs and moors like sentries, ready to burst into flame and give the alarm that would call up England's defenders the moment an enemy sail was sighted. But the rumor proved false.

Elizabeth had able naval commanders. The Lord Admiral was the competent, trustworthy Lord William Howard, no seafaring man but a landsman who nevertheless had learned all he could of seafaring and knew every inch of his ships from stem to stern and keel to maintop. The Queen also had bold and daring Vice Admiral Sir Francis Drake, the great sea fighter Rear Admiral Sir John Hawkins, the explorer and sailorman Captain Martin Frobisher and many others.

Hawkins was building a new type of galleon—longer and slimmer, with the old-style, high forecastles and sterncastles lowered to make the warships faster, more easily handled and able to mount more cannon. Sir William Wynter was arming them, substituting for iron guns the better brass culverins and demiculverins, with greater gun ranges and ship-smashing power.

That was the chief difference between the English fleet and the Armada. The old Spanish galleons were powerful, but slow and not easily maneuverable; their cannon were short and stubby, murderous but of short range. The Spaniards counted on closing in, battering their targets and then boarding them for hand-to-hand combat. The deep draft of these enemy galleons was finally to put an end to the Spanish Armada.

Drake and Hawkins wanted the Queen to send the galleons to bottle up the Spanish warships in port and thus prevent the Armada's sailing. The Queen said no. The admirals cursed this decision, but it turned out to be great wisdom. It cost a great deal of money to keep warships manned. On sea voyages vessels were often lost, and always, on their return, they needed expensive repairs and refitting. As for the men, who had to be paid and fed, they lived under unsanitary conditions, ate salt beef and weevil-infested biscuits and fell ill of diseases that killed many.

Elizabeth let the admirals stew. By the time the Armada was first sighted off the Scilly Islands at the entrance to the Channel, the English fleet was ready for sea and in prime shape for action.

That was on July 29, 1588. The captain of a warship cruising with others off the Channel came into Plymouth to find Sir Francis Drake, so legend has it, playing at bowls. Drake, about to send his ball rolling down the bowling green, stopped only long enough to say, "We have time enough to finish the game and beat the Spaniards too."

Probably Drake did finish his game. It was night when the

English warships began to warp out of Plymouth harbor and morning when Lord Admiral Howard in his flagship, the *Ark Royal*, led fifty-four warships out to meet the Spanish Armada.

The greatest sea battle of its time was a running fight that lasted six days. For one thing, the Armada's battle formation baffled the English, for it was something new. Howard's fleet came on in a long line, but the Spaniards were formed in a kind of rough crescent, with the most powerful galleons at the ends.

With both sides cannonading furiously, the English struck at each end of the crescent, but neither combatant suffered much damage. And it was suicidal for the English ships to try to break the Spanish line by striking at its middle. The Spaniards could surround the attacking ships, close in and do far more damage with their short, stubby cannon than the English guns, built for long range.

The English were worried. The Armada was bigger and stronger than they had expected. They had destroyed no important part of it, and the unbroken crescent was still sailing toward the rendezvous with Parma.

Medina Sidonia was even more worried. His enormous supply of powder was dwindling, and many of his vessels had no cannonballs of useful size left. He sent an urgent message to Parma for more, though so far he had heard nothing at all from the general. Meanwhile, the English were getting new supplies of ammunition from ashore, as well as reinforcements, while the Spanish commander could replace none of his many killed and wounded men.

Moreover, the English held the weather gauge—lying to windward of the Spaniards, an important advantage in battles between sailing ships. So the admiral suddenly signaled his fleet

173

to anchor off Calais, hoping the English, taken by surprise, would be swept past by wind and tide, giving the Armada the weather gauge. But the English were not fooled. They too anchored—to windward.

Lord Admiral Howard then held a war council. Dunkirk lay less than thirty miles away. Now, if ever, the Armada had to be stopped. It was agreed that there was only one way to do it— fireships.

They recruited a fleet of six vessels of from ninety to two hundred tons in size to be sacrificed. These were stuffed with everything possible that would burn, and their guns were double-shotted; they would fire when the flames heated the gun barrels red-hot.

Meanwhile, what was Parma doing? He had long ago written to tell Philip why he might not be able to join Medina Sidonia, but the admiral had not heard of it. The water off Dunkirk was so shallow that the deep-draft galleons of the Armada would have to anchor several leagues out. But the lighter-draft English warships could anchor closer to shore, cut off Parma's soldier-laden barges and sink them like sitting ducks. The English fleet had to be put out of action, or Parma could not venture out.

Medina Sidonia suspected that the English might send fireships against him. He set up a screen of small vessels in front of his warships to seize the fireships with grappling irons and tow them out of the way.

About midnight of August 6, the Spaniards saw the fireships in the distance, drifting down on the Armada before a strong wind. The screen of small vessels worked heroically, towing away two of the blazing fireships, but when the double-shotted guns in the other four began firing, the screen was driven off in confusion.

There was panic aboard the Armada. One warship went aground; the rest scattered in all directions. The English took after them, but the next day the Spanish ships reassembled and fought Howard's ships desperately. Save for a sudden change of wind they would all have been driven upon a graveyard of many ships in the shallow water off the Flanders coast.

Then, at a council of war, the Spaniards took stock of their severely damaged ships, almost exhausted ammunition and declining stocks of food and water, whose condition and amount had not been improved by those casks of green wood. They dared not try to sail home through the English Channel, so they took the long, dangerous route around the north coast of Scotland and south from there toward Spain, hoping to obtain food and water somehow along the way.

The rest of the story is one of disaster. The ships, many leaky or crippled by English gunfire, staggered far north, then west and south. Many were dashed to pieces on the reefs and rocky coasts of Scotland and Ireland, and thousands of men drowned. Landing parties in search of food and water in wild western Ireland were either butchered by the inhabitants or turned over to the English authorities. Fewer than seventy ships finally reeled into Spanish ports during that fall of 1588.

The Armada's defeat was the greatest achievement of Elizabeth's reign, and she had an important part in the English triumph. Yet the Queen found it most difficult to take part in the overwhelming celebrations that followed the victory. On September 4, 1588, Robert Dudley, Earl of Leicester, died of a fever. For thirty years her "Robin," as she called him, had been the closest of all her lovers. They had disagreed now and then, but Leicester had always been restored to favor. The Queen's grief was deep.

The earlier lovers of her reign now belonged to the past. They and her courtiers had bestowed many names upon her designed to glorify and flatter her—the Sun Queen; Cynthia, the moon goddess; Oriana, after a romantic, legendary English figure; Deborah, the biblical prophetess; Gloriana. Upon her admirers she in turn had bestowed droll nicknames. And even now, in spite of her age and faded beauty, there were those who professed to love her. Two stand out—Robert Devereux, Earl of Essex, and Sir Walter Raleigh. Raleigh is best known because of his voyages to Virginia in the New World, and the famous story of how he spread his velvet cloak over a mud puddle in the Queen's path. Most historians ignore the story and put it in a class with the legend of George Washington and the cherry tree. Yet Raleigh was just the sort to do such a gallant act, and it has never been proved that he did not do it. His black eyes, auburn hair and tall, powerful build all made this dashing man irresistible to the ladies. Except for a few quarrels, especially when the Queen caught him in other love affairs, he stood high in her favor from about 1581 until her death.

But the romantic and exciting story of Essex's love affair with Elizabeth outshines Raleigh's. He was Leicester's stepson, and at twenty-two became the great royal favorite after Leicester's death. He too was a tall, dashing young man with auburn hair.

He professed to love the Queen, and she adored him; yet they fought continually and as fiercely as a starved alley cat and a hungry mongrel over a piece of meat. They fought over Essex's secret marriage in 1590, over his love affairs with lovely young maids of honor at the Court, over this and over that; yet always, until Essex's last, unforgivable offense, he was restored to favor.

In 1596 Essex shared the glory of a daring reprisal for the Enterprise with Lord Admiral Howard. With Raleigh accompanying them, they destroyed a Spanish fleet in Cadiz harbor, sacked the city and brought back booty worth £13,000. Essex and the Queen fought over that too. Elizabeth calmly took all the money, and while Essex was furious, that quarrel too was soon forgotten.

Even when Essex did something that would undoubtedly have cost another man his head, Elizabeth let it pass. During a quarrel, Essex offered the Queen the usually unforgivable insult of turning his back on her. When she boxed his ears and cried, "Go to the devil!" the fiery Essex clapped his hand on his sword before others in the room could seize him.

Yet instead of sending him to the scaffold, the Queen dispatched him to Ireland to put down a serious rebellion there. Instead, Essex dallied, finally signed a humiliating truce with the Irish rebels' leader and returned to England. But his only punishment was confinement for a time to his own house, and the taking away of Elizabeth's gift to him of the rich revenues from customs duties on imported sweet wines.

Now the fuming Essex developed a persecution complex, sure that his enemies were plotting to kill him. He may have been insane, for what he did seems like the act of a madman. He organized a conspiracy, planning to capture the Tower with his followers, force the Queen to appoint him Protector to rule in her stead during her old age and if necessary kill her. The secret of the plot was so poorly kept that the government soon knew all about it, and Essex was arrested.

A week later, Essex was tried and quickly condemned. Unflinchingly, though with a heavy heart, Elizabeth signed his death warrant. On February 25, 1601, at the age of thirty-four, Robert Devereux, Earl of Essex, was beheaded on the Tower Green. When it was done, the Queen wept bitterly.

Elizabeth I had not long to live now. Many of her old friends were already gone. In August, 1598, William Cecil, Lord Burghley, had died. For forty years this wise, far-seeing minister had served the Queen with a loyalty that never wavered. More than a little of the glory of Elizabeth's reign was his. Burghley's death left a lasting mark on her.

As the year 1603 approached, Elizabeth was nearing seventy. Her face was withered and haggard. Her once-beautiful red-gold hair was gray and scanty, replaced long before by wigs. She was tired, and had recurring spells of illness, though she stoutly refused medicine.

In January, 1603, the Queen left Whitehall for her favorite palace of Richmond, which she spoke of as a "warm box" to shelter her old age. There the death of Lady Nottingham, one of the most devoted of her ladies-in-waiting, plunged her into grief and apprehension of her own death. By mid-March it was plain that she could not live long.

All through her reign, Elizabeth had refused to name her successor, and she remained silent, even on her deathbed. Her ministers would have to choose—and they well knew whom she favored.

On March 23, 1603, Queen Elizabeth's condition was such

that it was plain she could not live many hours. All through that day the Archbishop of Canterbury waited in the palace for a summons. At about six in the evening it came. Elizabeth realized the time was near, and although she had lost the power of speech, she made signs to her ladies to have the archbishop come.

He asked the Queen questions about her faith, and she answered with signs to show her trust in God and her salvation. Soon afterward, England's greatest queen, Elizabeth I, fell asleep. At about three o'clock in the morning of March 24, 1603, she died, still peacefully sleeping. A courier galloped madly north for Edinburgh to tell the Protestant King James VI of Scotland, next in line for the English throne after the execution of his mother, Mary Queen of Scots, that he was also James I of England, first of the Stuart kings.

The Tudor era had begun well under Henry VII, then slumped into wastefulness, religious dissension, intrigue, treason, war and terror. Elizabeth I restored England to greatness. Not only was the kingdom prospering, but a period of vast advances in exploration, colonization and the arts had begun. Great writers, playwrights, poets and philosophers were living and writing —men like Shakespeare, Ben Jonson, Sir Francis Bacon and others. The time of the Tudors may well be called a Golden Age in England.

SUGGESTED FURTHER READINGS

There are many good biographies of Henry VIII and Elizabeth I, since they were the most famous of the Tudors, as well as on Mary I; there are fewer on Henry VII, Edward VI and Lady Jane Grey. Of these latter three rulers, R. L. Storey's *The Reign of Henry VII* (New York: Walker, 1968), Hester W. Chapman's *Lady Jane Grey* (Boston: Little, Brown, 1962) and the same author's *The Last Tudor King—a Study of Edward VI* (London: Jonathan Cape, 1958) are all excellent biographies.

Mary Tudor, by H. F. M. Prescott (New York, Macmillan, 1962) can be recommended among Mary I's biographies. As for Henry VIII and Elizabeth I, the list is almost endless, and mention will be made of only one of each of many excellent biographies and studies. A. F. Pollard's *Henry VIII* (New York, Harper & Row, 1966) is by a distinguished historian, and *Elizabeth the Great*, by Neville Williams (New York: E. P. Dutton, 1968), is one of many well-written biographies of the great queen.

For an extremely popular biography, exhaustively researched, Antonia Fraser's *Mary Queen of Scots* (New York: Delacorte Press, 1969) stands out among a number of good ones.

The best-known, most carefully researched book—and a very readable story—of the Spanish Armada is Garrett Mattingly's *The Armada* (Boston: Houghton Mifflin, 1959).

Among the more readily obtainable books on life in England at the time of the Tudors are *Life and Letters in Tudor and*

Stuart England, by Louis B. Wright and Virginia L. La Mar (Ithaca, N.Y.: Cornell University Press, 1962), and *The England of Elizabeth,* by A. L. Rowse (New York: Macmillan, 1951), though there are many other excellent sources. For those who would like to read the collected histories of the Protestant martyrs under Mary I, John Foxe's *Foxe's Book of Martyrs* (Boston: Little, Brown, 1965) is obtainable in many libraries.

BIBLIOGRAPHY

Burton, Elizabeth. *The Pageant of Elizabethan England*. New York: Scribner, 1959.

Burton, William. *The Description of Leicestershire*. Lynn, England: W. Whittingham, 1777.

Byrne, M. St. Clare (editor). *The Letters of King Henry VIII*. New York: Funk & Wagnalls, 1968.

Carpenter, H. J. "Furse of Moreshead." Reports and Transactions of the Devonshire Association for the Development of Science, Literature and Art. Vol. 26, 1894.

Casson, Hugh (editor). *Castles*. New York: Taplinger, 1965.

Cave, Ann Estella. *Memories of Old Richmond*. London: John Murray, 1922.

Chapman, Hester W. *Lady Jane Grey*. Boston: Little, Brown, 1962.

———————— *The Last Tudor King—a Study of Edward VI*. London: Jonathan Cape, 1958.

Clair, Colin. *A Brief History of Westminster Abbey*. Watford, Herts.: Bruce and Gawthorn, c. 1968.

Constant, G. *The Reformation in England*. New York: Harper & Row, 1966.

Crossley, F. H. *The English Abbey*. London: B. T. Batsford, 1962.

Dark, Sidney. *Twelve Bad Men*. London: Hodder & Stoughton, 1928.

Bibliography

Dickens, A. G. *Thomas Cromwell and the English Reformation*. London: English Universities Press, 1959.

Ehrlich, Blake. *London on the Thames*. Boston: Little, Brown, 1966.

Fisher, Graham (editor). *Historic Britain*. Watford, Herts.: Oldhams Books, c. 1968.

Foxe, John. *Foxe's Book of Martyrs*. Boston: Little, Brown, 1965 (first published 1563).

Fraser, Antonia. *Mary Queen of Scots*. New York: Delacorte, 1969.

Fry, Plantagenet Somerset. *Rulers of Britain*. London: Paul Hamlin, 1967.

Girtin, T. Howard. *The Lord Mayors of London*. London: Oxford University Press, 1948.

Gwatkin, Henry Melville. *Religious Toleration in England* (Cambridge Modern History, Vol. 2). Cambridge University Press, 1903.

Hackett, Francis. *Henry the Eighth*. New York: Liveright, 1929.

Hanson, Michael. *2000 Years of London*. London: Country Life, 1967.

Harrison, G. B. (editor). *The Letters of Queen Elizabeth I*. New York: Funk & Wagnalls, 1968.

Harvey, John. *English Cathedrals*. London: B. T. Batsford, 1961.

Hoskins, William George. *Essays in Leicestershire History*. Liverpool University Press, 1950.

——————— *Midland England*. London: B. T. Batsford, 1949.

——————— *The Midland Peasant*. New York: St. Martin's Press, 1957.

——————— (editor). *The Victoria History of the Counties of England*. London: Oxford University Press, 1954.

Jenkins, Elizabeth. *Elizabeth the Great*. New York: Coward-McCann, 1959.

——————— *Elizabeth and Leicester*. New York: Coward-McCann, 1962.

Joseph, Richard. *Your Trip to Britain*. Garden City, N.Y.: Doubleday, 1954.

Levine, Joseph M. (editor). *Great Lives Observed: Elizabeth I*. Englewood Cliffs, N.J.: Prentice-Hall, 1969.

Luke, Mary M. *A Crown for Elizabeth*. New York: Coward-McCann, 1970.

Mackie, J. D. *The Earlier Tudors, 1485-1558* (Vol. 7, Oxford History of England). Oxford: Clarendon Press, 1952.

Mattingly, Garrett. *The Armada*. Boston: Houghton Mifflin, 1959.

Morrison, N. Bryson. *Mary Queen of Scots*. New York: Vanguard, 1960.

Neale, J. E. *Queen Elizabeth*. New York: Harcourt, Brace, 1934.

Parkes, Joan. *Travel in England in the Seventeenth Century*. London: Oxford University Press, 1925.

Pitt, Derek. *Henry VII*. London: Oxford University Press, 1966.

Pollard, A. F. *Henry VIII*. New York: Harper & Row, 1966.

——————— *Wolsey—Church and State in Sixteenth Century England*. New York: Harper & Row, 1966.

Prescott, H. F. M. *Mary Tudor*. New York: Macmillan, 1962.

Quennell, Marjorie and C. H. B. *A History of Everyday Things in England*. London: B. T. Batsford, 1950.

Ramsey, L. G. G. (editor). *The Connoisseur Year Book.* London: The Connoisseur, 1953.

Rowse, A. L. *Bosworth Field.* Garden City: Doubleday, 1966.

———————— *The England of Elizabeth.* New York: Macmillan, 1951.

———————— *The Expansion of Elizabethan England.* New York: Harper & Row, 1965.

Scarisbrick, J. J. *Henry VIII.* Berkeley: University of California Press, 1968.

Sitwell, Edith. *The Queens and the Hive.* Boston: Little, Brown, 1962.

Smith, Goldwin. *A History of England.* New York: Scribner, 1966.

Smith, Lacey Baldwin. *The Elizabethan World.* Boston: Houghton Mifflin, 1967.

Snell, Frederick John. *The Chronicles of Twyford (Tiverton, Devonshire).* London: Elliot Stock, 1892.

Stephen, Leslie and Lee, Sidney. *Dictionary of National Biography.* London: Oxford University Press. 1960.

Storey, R. L. *The Reign of Henry VII.* New York: Walker, 1968.

Stow, John. *The History and Survey of the Cities of London and Westminster.* London: Printed for M. Cooper, etc., 1754.

Strachey, Lytton. *Elizabeth and Essex.* New York: Harcourt, Brace, 1928.

Taylor, Duncan. *The Elizabethan Age.* London: Dennis Dobson, 1961.

Treharne, R. F. and Fullard, Harold. *Muir's New School Atlas of Universal History.* New York: Barnes & Noble, 1961.

Trevelyan, G. M. *England in the Age of Wycliffe, 1368-1520*. New York: Harper & Row, 1963.

Williams, Charles. *Henry VII*. London: Arthur Barker, 1937.

Williams, Neville. *Elizabeth the First, Queen of England*. New York: E. P. Dutton, 1968.

Woodward, G. W. O. *The Dissolution of the Monasteries*. New York: Walker, 1967.

Wright, Louis B., and La Mar, Virginia L. *Life and Letters in Tudor and Stuart England*. Ithaca: Cornell University Press, 1962.

Zweig, Stefan. *Mary Queen of Scotland and the Isles*. New York: Viking Press, 1935.

The Tower of London. London: Her Majesty's Stationery Office, 1967.

INDEX

Adrian VI, Pope, 54, 55
Alençon, Duke of, 148
Arne of Cleves, 75-76, 77
Archbishop of Canterbury, 48
Ark Royal, 173

Bacon, Sir Francis, 179
Bale, John, 15-16
Banbury, 21
Beaufort, Margaret, 20
Bedford, Duke of, *see* Jasper
 Tudor
Belknap, Edward, 37
Bloody Statutes, 74
Blundell, Peter, 9-15, 16
Boleyn, Anne, 56-66, 69-71, 72,
 77, 78, 102, 118, 119, 120, 141
Boleyn, Sir Thomas, 70
Bosworth Field, 24, 25, 29, 41
Bothwell, Earl of, 154-157
Brittany, 22, 23, 29
Buckingham, Duke of, 22-23, 48
Burghley, Lord, 144, 147, 157,
 165, 178
Burton Overy, 16

Cabot, John, 40
Cadiz, 168, 177
Calais, 9, 48, 54, 70, 80, 139, 174

Cambridge University, 15, 63,
 85, 134
Carlton Curlieu, 15, 16
Casket Letters, 157, 158
Catherine of Aragon, 41, 45, 46-
 48, 53, 56, 57, 58-61, 63, 69,
 72, 117, 118, 119, 124, 135,
 147
Cecil, Sir William, *see* Lord
 Burghley
Chamberlain, Lord, *see* Lord
 Thomas Stanley
Chapuys, Eustace, 119
Charles V, Emperor, 54, 55, 59,
 74, 79, 94, 95, 119, 121
Charles VIII, King, 23
Cheapside, 13, 47
Christina of Milan, Duchess, 74,
 75
Clement VII, Pope, 55, 58-60,
 63, 65, 66
Cleves, Duke of, 76
Columbus, Christopher, 40
Cornwall, 27, 30
Courtenay, Edward, 124, 125,
 138
Cranmer, Thomas, 63-65, 70, 78,
 81-82, 83, 91, 92, 104, 135

Index

Valois, Catherine of, 20
Vannes, 23
Venice, 53, 64

Wales, 20, 21, 24, 39, 73, 117, 125
Walsingham, Sir Francis, 159-160, 163
Wars of the Roses, 20, 22, 24, 25, 31
Warbeck, Perkin, 29, 30

Warham, William, 57, 58-59
Westminster, 14, 34, 47, 122, 162
Westminster Abbey, 24, 28, 38, 47, 48, 65, 87, 104, 124, 145
White Tower, 14
Whitehall Palace, 14, 146
Windsor Castle, 13, 73, 82, 91, 94
Wolsey, Cardinal Thomas, 43, 50-56, 57, 58-63, 64
Wyatt, Sir Thomas, 125-128, 132, 137

ABOUT THE AUTHOR

Clifford Lindsey Alderman was born in Springfield, Massachusetts and graduated from the United States Naval Academy at Annapolis. Much of his subsequent career was as an editor and in public relations work in the field of shipping and foreign trade, but during World War II he returned to naval service.

Mr. Alderman has written historical novels for adults and both fiction and non-fiction for young people. He believes in knowing firsthand the places of which he writes and has traveled extensively in Europe, Canada, the West Indies, and throughout the United States.

He lives with his wife in Seaford, New York.